From Your Friends At The MAILBOX

23 Ready-To-Go Lesson Plans

SCIENCE

GRADE 1

www.themailbox.com

What Are Lifesaver Lessons®?

Lifesaver Lessons® are well-planned, easy-to-implement, curriculum-based lessons. Each lesson contains a complete materials list, step-by-step instructions, a reproducible activity or pattern, and several extension activities.

How Do I Use A Lifesaver Lesson?

Each Lifesaver Lesson is designed to decrease your preparation time and increase the amount of quality teaching time with your students. These lessons are great for introducing or reinforcing new concepts. You may want to look through the lessons to see what types of materials to gather. After completing a lesson, be sure to check out the fun-filled extension activities.

What Materials Will I Need?

Most of the materials for each lesson can be easily found in your classroom or school. Check the list of materials below for any items you may need to gather or purchase.

- crayons
- pencils
- scissors
- markers
- glue
- tape
- rulers
- writing paper
- construction paper
- drawing paper
- chart paper
- bulletin-board paper
- blank transparencies
- transparency markers
- overhead projector
- stapler
- index cards
- game markers
- paper clips
- nonbreakable cups
- pennies, nickels, and dimes
- clipboards or other portable writing surfaces
- marbles or dried beans
- paper lunch bag
- hole puncher
- clear container with wide lid
- tacks
- craft sticks
- sticky notes
- chalk and chalkboard eraser
- brads
- cotton balls
- black or gray powdered tempera paint
- book in fairly poor condition
- thermometers
- paper towels
- yarn
- rocks
- keys
- string
- discarded magazines
- rubber bands
- materials to demonstrate simple machines
- mirror(s)
- small containers
- magnets
- iron nails, metal spoons, screws, aluminum foil
- seed packet

Project Editor:
Sharon Murphy

Writers:
Elizabeth Almy, Catherine Broome, Darcy Brown, Lisa Buchholz, Amy Erickson, Jill Hamilton, Lisa Kelly, Sharon Murphy, Sandy Shaw, Susan Hohbach Walker

Artists:
Jennifer Tipton Bennett, Clevell Harris, Sheila Krill, Mary Lester, Rob Mayworth, Kimberly Richard, Barry Slate

Cover Artist:
Jennifer Tipton Bennett

Table Of Contents

www.themailbox.com

ISBN #1-56234-242-8

Manufactured in the United States
10 9 8 7 6 5

What's Alive?

Take your young scientists and head outside to find and observe living and nonliving things!

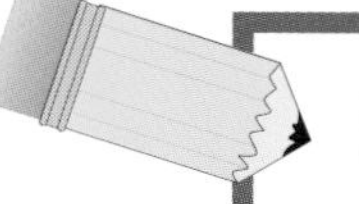

Skill: Identifying living and nonliving things

Estimated Lesson Time: 45 minutes

Teacher Preparation:

1. Divide a sheet of chart paper into two columns. Label one column "Living" and the other column "Nonliving."
2. Duplicate page 5 for each student.

Materials:

1 sheet of chart paper labeled "Living" and "Nonliving"
1 sheet of writing paper for each group of four students
1 pencil per student group
1 clipboard or other portable writing surface per group
1 copy of page 5 for each student
crayons

Background Information:

- *Living things* need water, food, and air.
- *Living things* can grow, change, and reproduce.
- There are more than 10 million different species of *living things* on earth.
- *Living things* can be found in different environments.
- All *living things* are made up of cells.

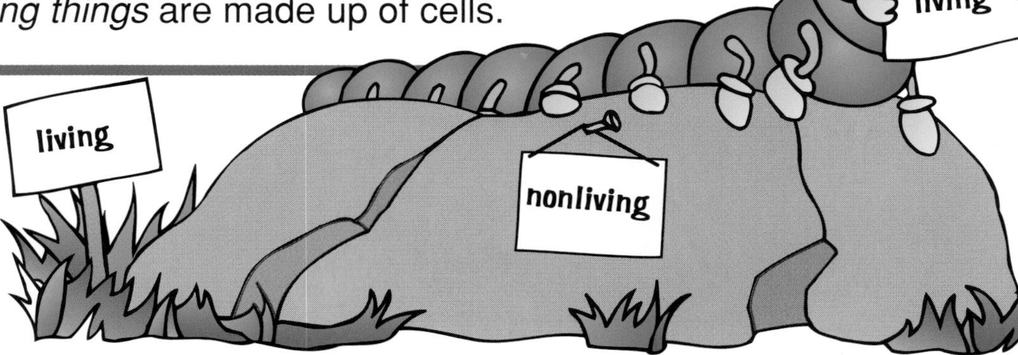

Introducing The Lesson:

Ask students what they have in common with a tree. Lead them to the conclusion that trees and people both are living things. Then tell students that they are going to search the schoolyard for examples of living and nonliving things.

Steps:

1. Use the Background Information on page 3 to discuss with students the characteristics of all living things. Enlist students' help in naming examples of both living and nonliving things.

2. Divide the class into groups of four students and assign a recorder in each group. Give each group a sheet of writing paper, a pencil, and a clipboard to use as a writing surface.

3. Take students outside and instruct each group to find and record as many living and nonliving things as possible in a predetermined amount of time.

4. After returning to the classroom, have a student from each group share the items that his group recorded for each category. Discuss each item and its characteristics; then record the responses under the appropriate heading (living or nonliving) on the chart paper.

5. Distribute crayons and a copy of page 5 to each student.

6. Challenge students to complete the Bonus Box activity.

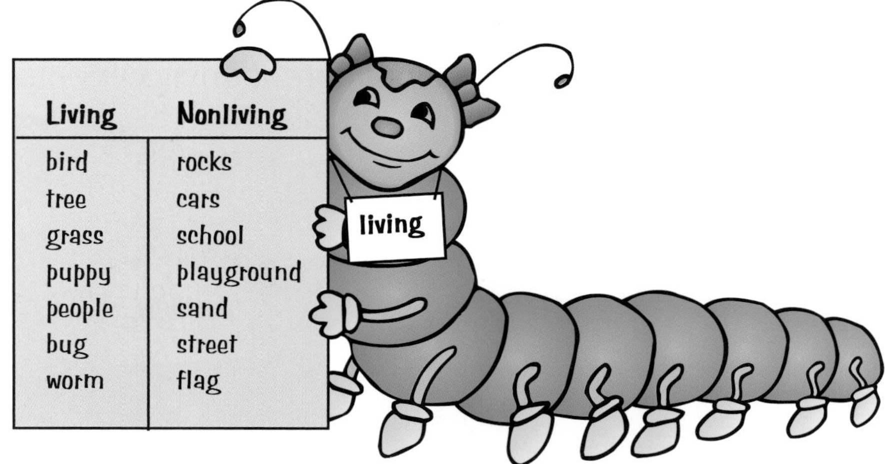

Name ______________________________

What's Alive?

Color all the living things green.
Color all the nonliving things blue.

Bonus Box: On the back of this sheet, draw a picture of the classroom. Color all the living things green. Color all the nonliving things blue.

How To Extend The Lesson:

- Have your students create murals featuring living and nonliving things. To begin, divide students into small groups and assign each group a location such as the beach, school, or park. Also provide each group with a large sheet of bulletin-board paper, crayons, scissors, glue, and construction paper. Have each group create a mural of its designated location that includes a variety of living and nonliving things that could be found there. When the murals are complete, post them on a classroom wall. Then have students take turns labeling the items as either "living" or "nonliving."

- Create a living/nonliving classification center. To make the center, cut pictures of living and nonliving things from discarded magazines. Laminate the pictures; them store them in a large envelope at a center. Instruct students to visit the center in small groups and sort each picture into its appropriate category—living or nonliving.

- Invite students to play the game 20 Questions. Choose one student volunteer to think of a person or an object in the classroom. Instruct the other children to first ask the question, "Is it living?" or, "Is it nonliving?" After the volunteer answers, have students continue to ask other yes or no questions until the correct answer is guessed or 20 questions have been asked. If 20 questions have been asked and no one has guessed the correct answer, ask the student volunteer to reveal the secret item.

- Use the chart made in the lesson (see page 4) to remind students of the living and nonliving things they saw outside. Then have students make a class book describing these items. In advance program the bottom of a sheet of white paper with the sentence "An [item from chart] is [living or nonliving] because [reason]." Distribute a copy of the page to each child. Instruct each student to choose a different item from the list created in the lesson and complete his sentence. (For example, a student may write "A flag is nonliving because it cannot grow.") Have students illustrate their sentences. Staple the completed pages between two construction-paper covers and add the title "What's Alive In The Schoolyard?"

Hootin'-Good Science

"Whoo's" wise about science? Your students, that's "whoo"! Reinforce the current science topic with this review activity.

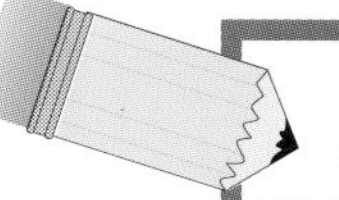

Skill: Reviewing a science topic

Estimated Lesson Time: 30 minutes

Teacher Preparation:

1. Duplicate page 9 for each student.
2. Enlarge and duplicate page 9. Color and cut out the owl.

Materials:

1 copy of page 9 per student
1 colored owl cutout
crayons
scissors

Teacher Tip:

Incorporate this activity into your unit of study by using it to

- assess student understanding of the topic
- help students review before a test
- reinforce key unit vocabulary
- incorporate writing skills with science
- encourage students to contribute a personal response to learning

Introducing The Lesson:

Show students the colored owl cutout. Tell students that his name is Professor Owl and he would like to know some information about the current science topic they are studying (or about a unit previously studied).

Steps:

1. Ask students to brainstorm desired information about the science topic. Write students' responses on the chalkboard—at least one response per student.

2. Give each student a copy of page 9. On the owl's tummy have each student write at least three facts from the chalkboard.

3. Next have her color, personalize, and cut out the owl.

4. Display the owls and Professor Owl on a bulletin board titled " 'Whoo's' Wise About [designated science topic]?"

Pattern

Use with Steps 2, 3, and 4 on page 8.

How To Extend The Lesson:

- Invite a specialist in the current science topic to visit the classroom and speak to your students. The day before the visit, have youngsters brainstorm questions about the topic that they would like to ask the specialist. Write the questions on a sheet of chart paper; then post the list on the chalkboard. On the day of the visit, provide time for students to choose a question to ask the special visitor. As a follow-up to the visit, have students write thank-you letters to the specialist.

- Enlist students' help in making a science-review game. Provide each student with an index card. Have each student write a question about the present science topic on one side of her card. Then ask her to write the answer to the question and her name on the other side of the card. Collect the completed cards and divide the students into two teams. Before beginning remind students that they cannot answer their own questions. To play the game, read a question and call on a student volunteer from one of the teams to answer the question. If she answers correctly, award her team one point. If she answers incorrectly, call on a student volunteer from the other group to answer. Award one point to her team for a correct answer. If both teams answer incorrectly, have the student who wrote the question give the answer (no points awarded). Continue asking questions to alternating teams until all the questions have been asked. The team with the most points wins!

- Have students write letters to their parents or friends explaining interesting facts they learned with the current science topic.

- Enlist students' help in performing an experiment to conclude the topic of study. Ask students the questions shown below as you lead them through the experiment.

> - *Purpose:* What do you want to find out?
> - *Prediction:* What do you think will happen?
> - *Materials:* What items do you need in order to do this experiment?
> - *Procedure:* What steps will you follow?
> - *Observations:* What happened during this experiment?
> - *Conclusion:* What did you learn from this experiment?

Plants With Pizzazz

No doubt students' science skills will grow with this lesson on plant parts!

Skill: Identifying the parts of a plant

Estimated Lesson Time: 25 minutes

Teacher Preparation:

1. Divide a sheet of chart paper into four columns. Label one column for each of the following plant parts: "leaves," "fruits and seeds," "stems," and "roots."
2. Duplicate page 13 for each student.

Materials:

1 sheet of chart paper
1 copy of page 13 per student
crayons
scissors
glue

Background Information:

There are more than 375,000 different types of plants. Flowering plants form the largest group. These plants have four main parts: roots, stems, leaves, and flowers.

Roots: A plant is anchored into soil by its roots. From the soil, roots take in the water and minerals that a plant needs to grow. Some roots store food, too.
Stem: The stem of a plant helps transport water and minerals. It also holds the plant up to the light, supporting its flowers and leaves.
Leaves: Most plants have green leaves because they contain green pigment called *chlorophyll.* The chlorophyll absorbs light; then the energy from the light helps plants make food. During this process, known as *photosynthesis,* plants give off oxygen. Without plants there would not be enough oxygen in the air for us to survive.
Flower: The reproductive parts of a flowering plant are contained in its flowers. The bright colors, markings, and scents of flowers attract insects for *pollination*—the process of making seeds. A plant's seeds are protected by the fruit that grows around them. All flowering plants have fruit.

Introducing The Lesson:

Tell youngsters that lettuce, sunflowers, celery, and carrots have features in common. Ask students to name as many of these shared characteristics as they can. Then explain that one of the most important traits these plants share is that each of them has at least one edible part. Announce that students will learn more about the parts of plants with this lesson.

Steps:

1. Point out that edible plant parts include leaves, fruits and seeds, stems, and roots; then share the Background Information on page 11.

2. Invite students to brainstorm edible plants, and challenge them to identify which part(s) of each of these plants we eat. Record youngsters' responses by writing the name of each plant in the appropriate column(s) on the chart.

3. Explain that each student will complete a plant diagram. Then give each youngster a copy of page 13.

4. Have each student cut out the words at the bottom of his sheet and glue them in the appropriate locations. Then direct him to personalize his work.

5. Challenge students to complete the Bonus Box activity.

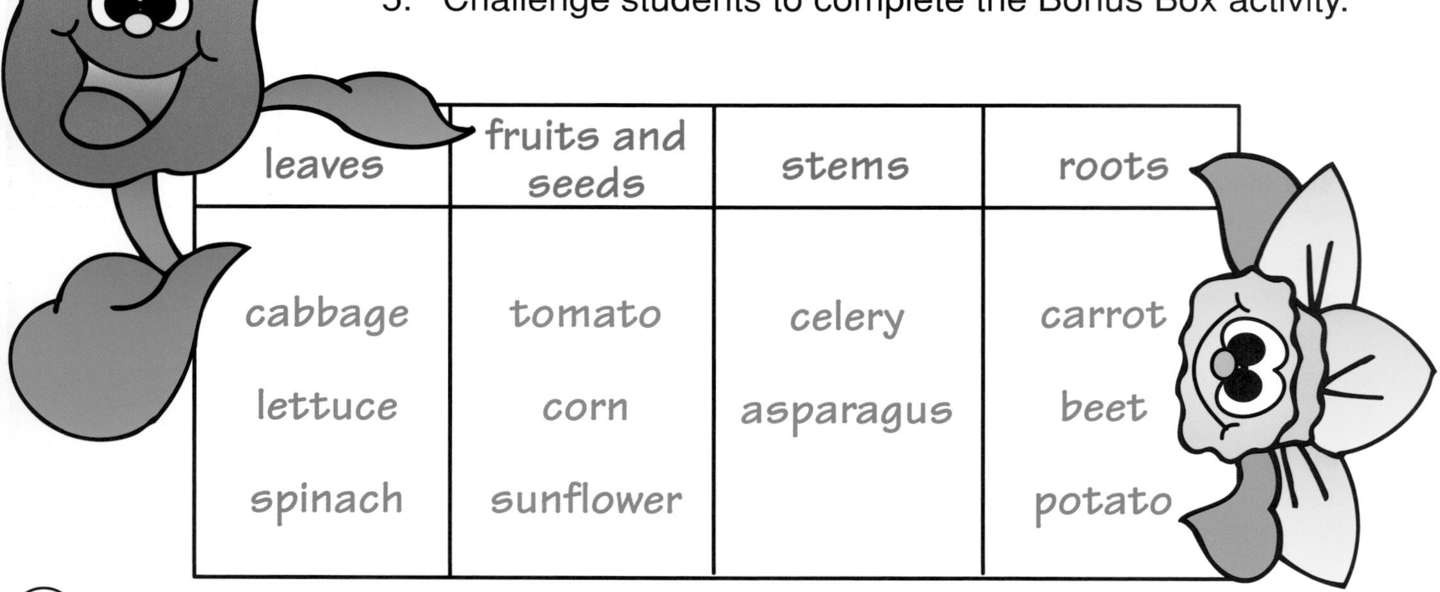

leaves	fruits and seeds	stems	roots
cabbage	tomato	celery	carrot
lettuce	corn	asparagus	beet
spinach	sunflower		potato

Name ____________________ *Identifying the parts of a plant*

Plants With Pizzazz

Cut.
Glue.
Color.

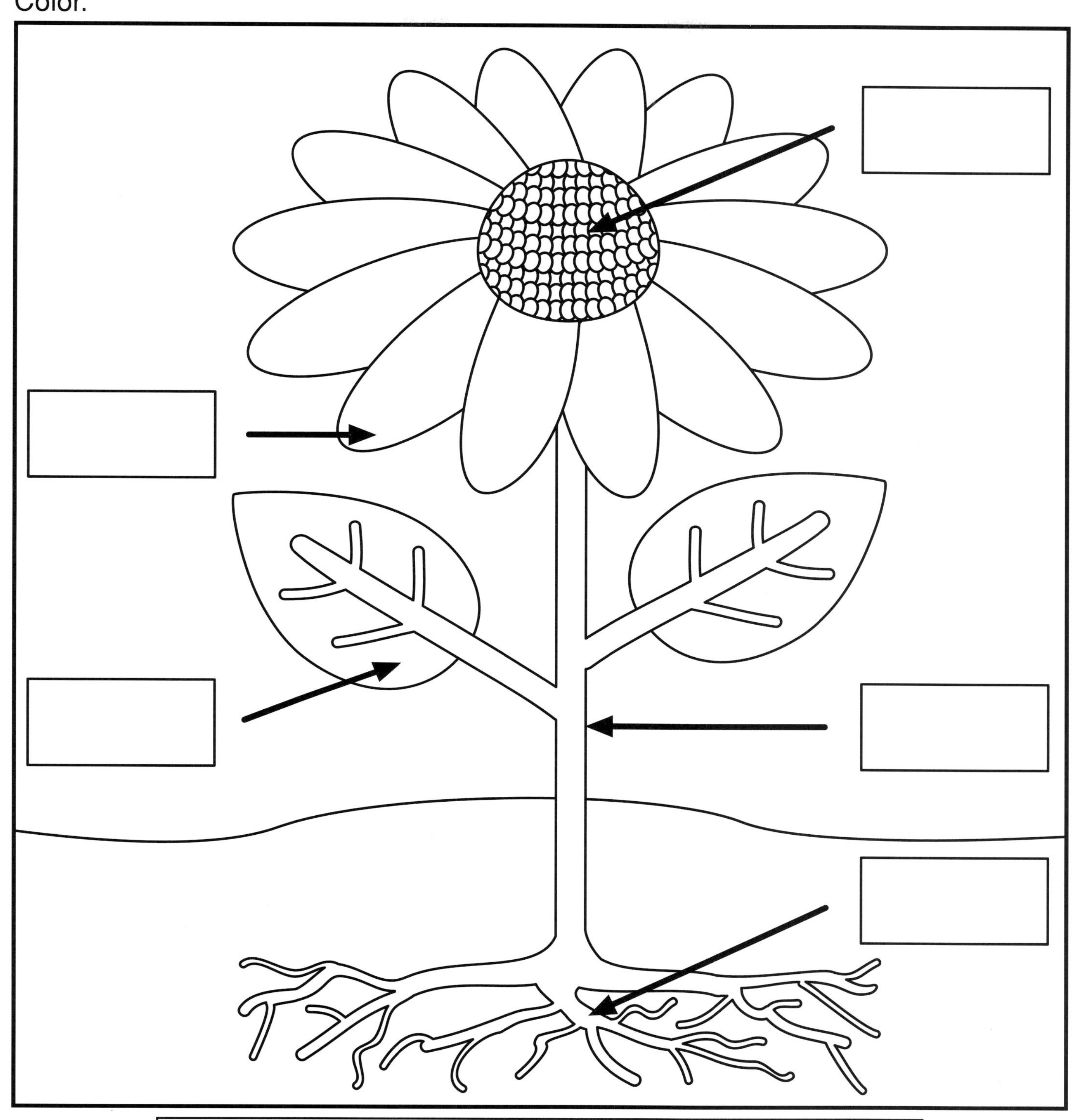

Bonus Box: On the back of this sheet, write two reasons that plants are important.

leaf	roots	seeds	stem	flower

How To Extend The Lesson:

- Enlist students' help in planting a classroom window garden. You might have each student plant seeds in a separate container, such as an empty milk carton or a Styrofoam® cup, or have students work together to plant seeds in window boxes. For best results, choose seeds that germinate quickly. Alfalfa seeds, lima beans, and marigolds are good choices. After the seeds have been planted, develop a watering schedule. Then, each day for a designated period of time, have each student describe and illustrate the plants' development in a journal. For added learning fun, experiment with the amount of light and water each plant receives and note the results.

- Your budding botanists will enjoy digging into these books about plants!
  —*Pearl's First Prize Plant* by A. Delaney (HarperCollins Children's Books, 1997)
  —*From Seed To Plant* by Gail Gibbons (Holiday House, Inc.; 1993)
  —*The Reason For A Flower* by Ruth Heller (The Putnam Publishing Group, 1983)
  —*The Rose In My Garden* by Arnold Lobel (Morrow Junior Books, 1993)

- Teach students about the plant-growing cycle with this story-retelling activity. First read aloud *The Tiny Seed* by Eric Carle (Simon & Schuster Children's Division, 1991). Then give each youngster a large construction-paper circle. Instruct him to fold the circle in half and then in half again. Have him open the circle and draw lines on the creases to divide his paper into quarters. Have him label the top of each quarter section with a different season as shown. Then ask each youngster to draw and write in each labeled quarter what happened to the tiny seed during the corresponding season. Remind youngsters that autumn returns after summer and the growing cycle begins again.

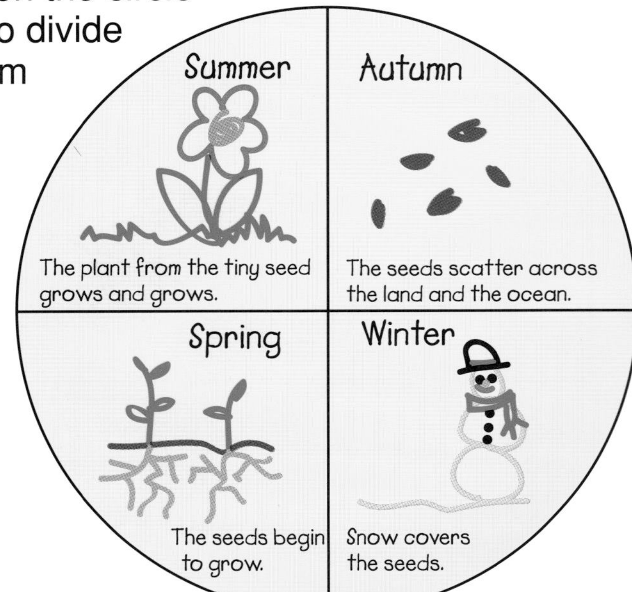

Plants And Their Needs

Put on those green thumbs and sow a garden of appreciation for the needs of plants!

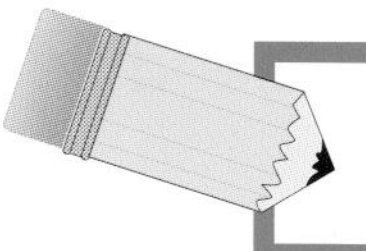

Skill: Understanding basic needs of plants

Estimated Lesson Time: 45 minutes

Teacher Preparation:

1. Duplicate page 17 for each student.
2. Re-create a copy of page 17 on a sheet of bulletin-board paper. Mount the paper in a prominent location.

Materials:

1 copy of page 17 per student
1 labeled sheet of bulletin-board paper
1 plant (optional)
at least one seed packet
markers or crayons
glue
hole puncher
yarn
tacks

Background Information:

- A plant's growth is shaped by both its heredity and its environment.
- A plant's heredity determines characteristics such as a flower's color and general size.
- Environmental factors include sunlight, climate, and soil condition. These factors affect the rate of growth, the size, and the reproduction of all plants.
- All plants need light, a suitable climate, and an ample supply of water and minerals from the soil.
- Plants differ in the amount of sunlight and water they need.

Introducing The Lesson:

Show students a plant. (Or tell them that you are thinking about buying a plant.) Then ask youngsters to explain what you need to do to take care of the plant. Write students' responses on the chalkboard. Then tell students they will be designing seed packets as they review the basic needs of plants.

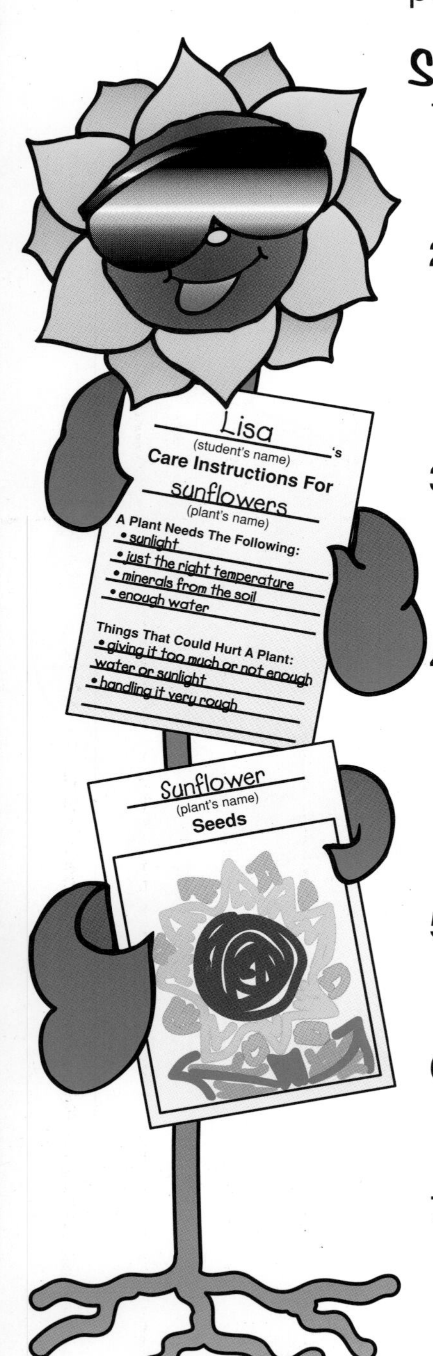

Steps:

1. Share the Background Information about the needs of plants (page 15). Then enlist students' help in making any necessary changes to the list on the chalkboard.
2. Tell students that although many plants grow from seeds, not all plants do. Explain that a plant may grow from any part of another plant—a root, stem, leaf, or flower. No matter what the plant grows from, it still has the same basic needs.
3. Show students the seed packet(s). Explain that people plant seeds mainly to grow flowers or vegetables. (Remind students that both flowers and vegetables are plants.)
4. Next use the displayed bulletin-board paper to show students how to create a seed packet. On the right side of the paper, write the name of a desired type of flower or vegetable. Next draw a picture of the plant in the provided box. On the left side of the paper, demonstrate how to complete the Care Instructions for any plant.
5. Distribute a copy of page 17 to each student. Have each student choose a flower or vegetable, then complete her seed packet as previously described.
6. Next have each student fold her paper on the dotted line, then glue the sides together (except the top) to create a packet.
7. When the glue has dried, hole-punch each packet and thread a length of yarn through the holes. Tie the yarn's ends; then tack the packet by the yarn to a bulletin board titled "Seeds And Their Needs."

____________________'s
(student's name)

Care Instructions For

____
(plant's name)

A Plant Needs The Following:

Things That Could Hurt A Plant:

____
(plant's name)

Seeds

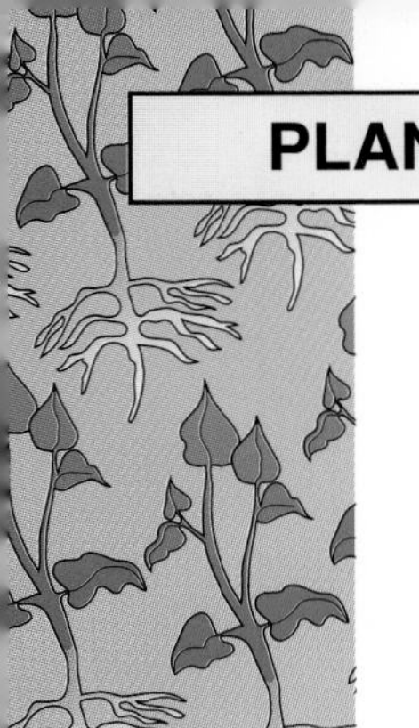

How To Extend The Lesson:

- Try this experiment to show students the importance of sunlight to green plants. Cover several leaves of a plant with aluminum foil. Place the plant in a sunny location. After several days, remove the foil and have students examine the leaves.

- The following experiment demonstrates the effect of temperature on the sprouting of seeds. Place four bean seeds and four radish seeds on a well-soaked paper towel. Wrap the seeds and paper towel in plastic wrap; then place the packet near a heater. Repeat the procedure, but this time place the packet in a refrigerator. Have students observe the seeds each day for a week. At the end of the week, ask students to compare the seeds in each packet. Lead students to the conclusion that seeds need a warm environment to sprout.

- Share some of these plentiful plant books:
  —*Plant And Flower* by David Burnie (Alfred A. Knopf Books For Young Readers, 1989)
  —*The Flower Alphabet Book* by Jerry Pallotta (Charlesbridge Publishing, Inc; 1989)
  —*Flowers, Trees, And Fruits* by Sally Morgan (Kingfisher LKC, 1996)
  —*The Plant-And-Grow Project Book* by Ulla Dietl (Sterling Publishing Company, Inc.; 1995)
  —*Plant Families* by Carol Levner (William Morrow And Company, Inc.; 1989)
  —*The Visual Dictionary Of Plants* (Dorling Kindersley Publishing, Inc.; 1992)

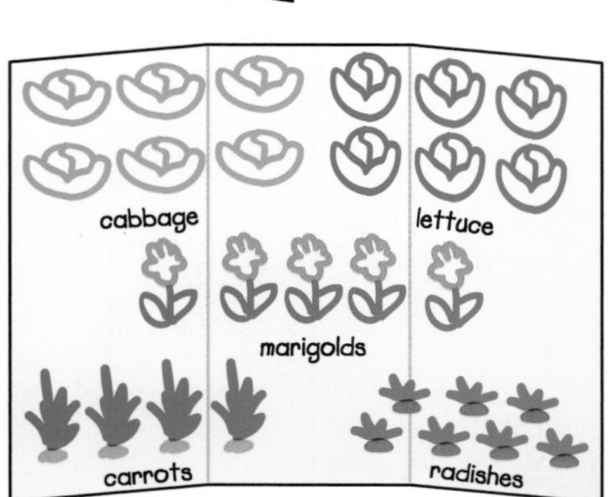

- This idea provides students with an opportunity to create imaginary indoor gardens. To begin, each student folds a 9" x 12" sheet of drawing paper widthwise into thirds. On the top flap, she writes her name and a list of the vegetables and/or flowers she would like to plant in her garden. Next she folds back that flap and writes the steps for caring for the garden on the other flap. After planning the vegetable and/or flower placements in her garden, she completely unfolds her paper and draws and labels her garden on the inside portion of the paper.

Classifying Critters

Your youngsters will classify this animal learning experience as fun!

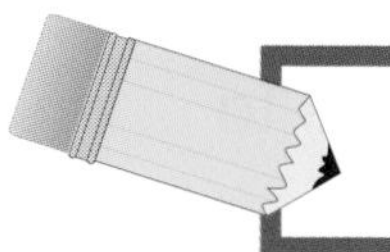

Skill: Classifying animals by attributes

Estimated Lesson Time: 45 minutes

Teacher Preparation:

1. Create several classification signs by writing a different animal group or characteristic on each of several 9" x 12" pieces of construction paper. Choose characteristics or groups such as four legs, no legs, fins, hair or fur, wings, shells, insects, reptiles, mammals, and amphibians.
2. Duplicate page 21 for each student.

Materials:

a set of animal classification signs
one 3" x 5" index card per student
1 copy of page 21 per student
tape

Background Information:

Some common ways animals can be grouped:

- according to whether or not they live on land (terrestrial animals) or in water (aquatic animals).
- by the number of legs they have
- by how they move (fly, swim, crawl, run, hop)
- according to whether they are cold-blooded or warm-blooded
- by whether they have backbones (vertebrates) or not (invertebrates)
- by whether they are pets or wild animals
- according to their skin coverings, such as fur or scales

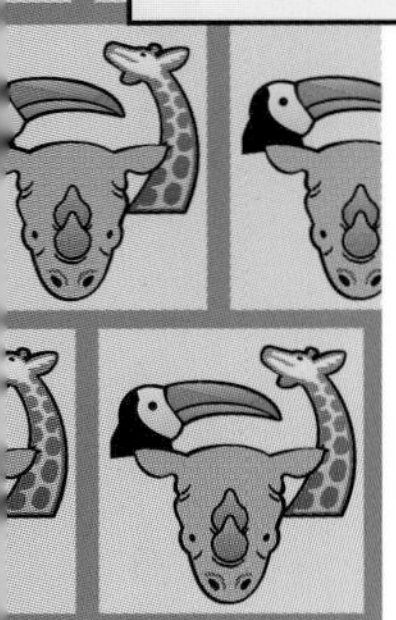

Introducing The Lesson:

Announce to your students that they are going to become famous animal explorers. Their job is to search for similarities and differences among animals. Explain to the students that these similarities and differences will provide many ways to classify the animals.

Steps:

1. Use the Background Information on page 19 to explain several different ways that animals can be grouped.
2. Ask students to brainstorm as many different animals as possible. Record students' responses on the chalkboard. Be sure the list includes animals from all different groups. (See the list below if needed.)
3. Distribute an index card to each student. Have each student choose a different animal from the list and illustrate it on his index card. Then tape each student's card to his shirt.
4. Display a classification sign for everyone to see. Ask students to decide whether the animals they drew have that characteristic. If they do, invite those students to stand by the characteristic sign. After checking those students' animal cards, have them return to their seats.
5. Repeat this activity several times using a new classification card each time.
6. Distribute a copy of page 21 to each student.
7. Challenge students to complete the Bonus Box activity.

Some animals classified by characteristics:
Critters With Fur: bears, tigers, lions, skunks, cats, dogs
Critters With Fins: guppies, tuna, catfish, goldfish, sharks, whales
Critters With Wings: flies, birds, mosquitoes, crickets, dragonflies, moths
Critters With Shells: snails, tortoises, lobsters, shrimp, crabs

Some animals classified by groups:
Amphibians: frogs, toads, salamanders, newts
Insects: ants, spiders, ladybugs, grasshoppers, butterflies, bees
Mammals: horses, gorillas, monkeys, mice, elephants, humans
Reptiles: snakes, turtles, alligators, lizards, dinosaurs, crocodiles

Name ______________________________

Classifying Critters

Cut and paste to match each animal to its group.
Complete each sentence.

1. They all ______________________________.

2. They all ______________________________.

3. They all ______________________________.

4. They all ______________________________.

Bonus Box: On the back of this sheet, draw and label four more animals—one for each group.

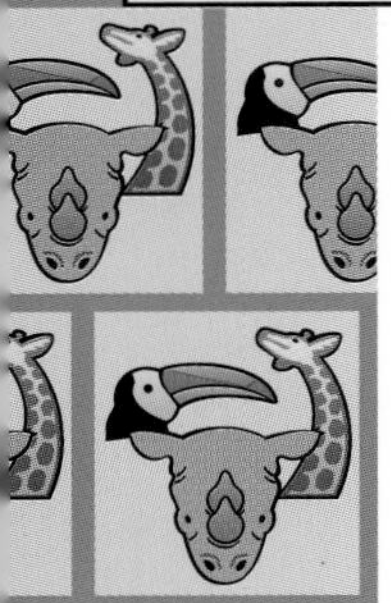

How To Extend The Lesson:

- Invite each student to bring a stuffed animal to school. Have students use the classification signs (from the lesson) to sort and classify the animals.

- Have students use Venn diagrams to classify a variety of animals. To begin divide students into groups of five. Provide each group with a poster-board-size Venn diagram and several paper strips, each labeled with a different animal characteristic. Have each group choose two labels and place each label above a circle on the diagram. Then have the group sort their animal cards (from the lesson) using the characteristics on the labels. After providing time for students to discuss how animals may have more than one characteristic, have them replace the labels with different ones and repeat the activity. Encourage groups to continue in this same manner until each label has been used at least once. For added fun have one student sort all of the cards by a desired characteristic, then challenge the rest of his group to guess the category.

- Have students create imaginary animals to sort and classify. Have each student draw an imaginary animal on a sheet of drawing paper. (For example a student may draw a picture of a dog with wings or a tiger with duck feet and fins.) Then announce an animal characteristic and have students raise their pictures if their animals have the announced characteristic. Repeat the activity several times. Provide time for students to share how many different groups their animals fit into.

- This sorting activity provides a great review of animal classification. Have each student fold a 12" x 18" sheet of construction paper in half, then fold it once more time to create four equal sections. Then instruct him to unfold his paper and label the top of each section with a different animal characteristic or group. Have each child cut animal pictures from discarded magazines and glue each picture under the appropriate section on his paper.

FINS
MAMMALS
INSECTS
HAIR OR FUR

What Changes!

Challenge your youngsters' life-cycle savvy with this review activity!

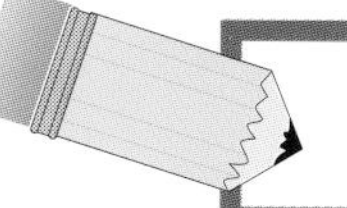

Skill: Sequencing life-cycle stages

Estimated Lesson Time: 30 minutes

Teacher Preparation:

1. Gather three or four photographs of yourself that span your lifetime from child- to adulthood. Or cut pictures from discarded magazines of a baby, a child, an adult, and a senior citizen.
2. Duplicate page 25 for each student.

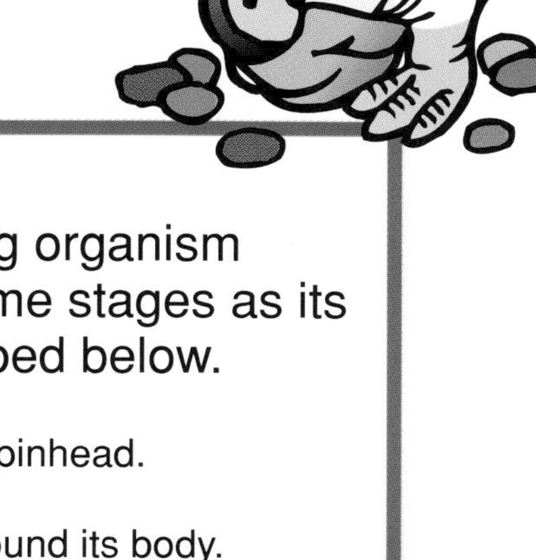

Materials:

1 copy of page 25 per student
4 craft sticks (or poster-board strips) per student
tape
scissors

Background Information:

A life cycle is a sequence of stages through which a living organism passes. Each member of a species goes through the same stages as its parents. The stages of two types of creatures are described below.

Monarch Butterfly:

1. On a milkweed plant, a monarch butterfly lays an egg the size of a pinhead.
2. A caterpillar hatches from the egg.
3. The caterpillar turns into a pupa. It forms a hard protective shell around its body.
4. The pupa opens and an adult butterfly emerges.

Emperor Penguin:

1. An emperor penguin lays an egg in winter. Instead of building a nest for the egg, the male and female penguins take turns holding their egg on their feet to keep it warm and safe.
2. A fluffy gray chick is born.
3. The chick grows into a young penguin and develops a coat of feathers. The young penguin spends its first few years at sea.
4. When it is about six years old, the penguin joins the adult flock.

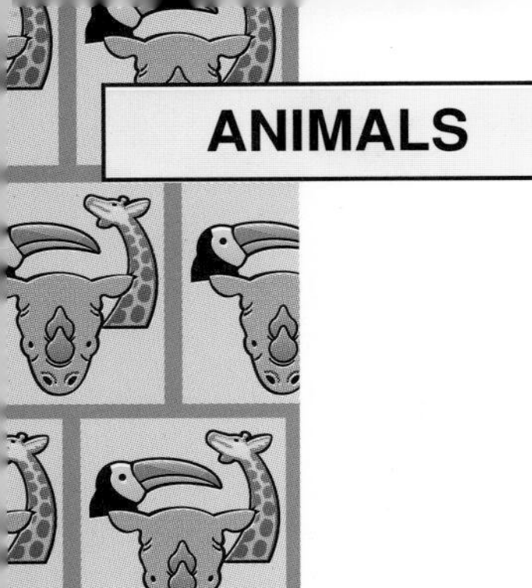

Introducing The Lesson:

Show students your photos (or the magazine pictures) and have youngsters sequence the pictures in chronological order on your chalkboard ledge. Explain to students that all living things pass through stages or life cycles as they grow.

Steps:

1. Ask students to brainstorm examples of how living things change as they grow. Record students' ideas on the chalkboard.

2. Use the Background Information on page 23 to define the term *life cycle;* then share the two life-cycle examples included in the Background Information.

3. Distribute a copy of page 25 to each student. Have students color and cut out the pictures of the monarch butterfly life cycle.

4. Give each child four craft sticks and have him tape each butterfly life-cycle picture onto a separate stick. Have students put aside the resulting stick puppets.

5. Next have students color and cut out the pictures of the penguin life cycle. Help each student tape these pictures onto the back of the butterfly stick puppets.

6. Pair students and have them place their puppets on their desks with the butterfly pictures showing. Instruct each student to use his puppets to explain the life cycle of a monarch butterfly to his partner. Then have him tell the life stages of a penguin in a similar manner.

7. Have youngsters take home the stick puppets and use them to explain the life cycles of butterflies and penguins to family members.

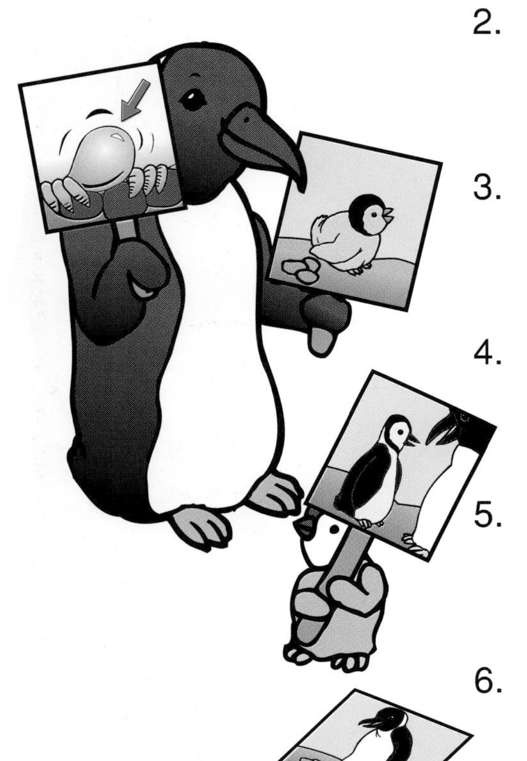

Name ______________________________

Color. Cut out. Sequence.
Tape each picture onto a craft stick.

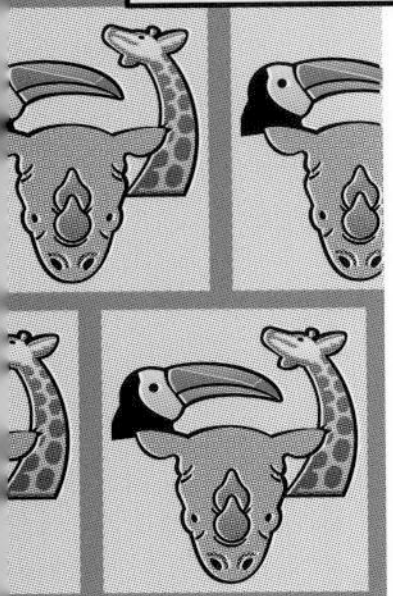

How To Extend The Lesson:

- Divide students into groups of three or four. Have each group role-play the life cycle of a different animal. If desired transform this role-playing exercise into a game of charades, and have the class audience guess each stage depicted.

- This small-group writing activity is perfect for reviewing the life cycle of a variety of animals. To begin divide students into small groups and assign each group a recorder and a desired animal. Each group creates a story about the life cycle of the animal from the animal's point of view. The recorder writes each stage on a separate sheet of story paper. Then each student illustrates (or helps illustrate) a different stage. Compile each group's completed work between two construction-paper covers. Ask each group to personalize its cover as desired, then share it with the class.

- Share with students these intriguing books about the life cycles of specific creatures:
  —*The Beaver* by Sabrina Crewe (Raintree Steck-Vaughn Publishers, 1998)
  —*Butterfly Story* by Anca Hariton (Dutton Children's Books, 1995)
  —*A Nest Full Of Eggs* by Priscilla Belz Jenkins (HarperCollins Children's Books, 1995)
  —*From Tadpole To Frog* by Wendy Pfeffer (HarperCollins Children's Books, 1994)
  —*Mouse* with photos by Barrie Watts (Dutton Children's Books, 1992)

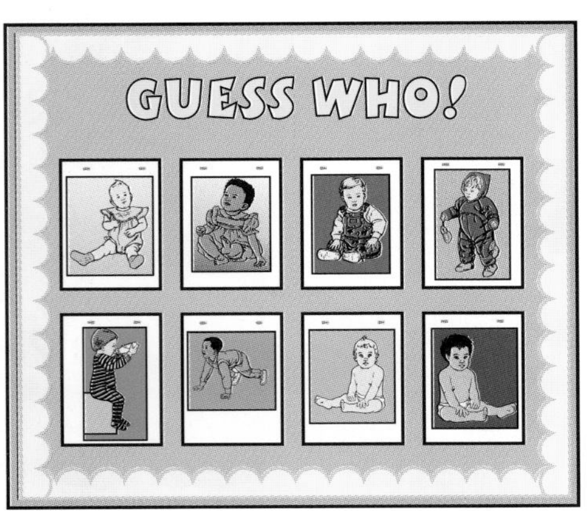

- Ask each student to bring one of his baby photos and a current photo of himself to school. Help him tape each photo onto a separate sheet of paper. Staple his baby photo page atop his current photo page. Mount each student's set of pages on a brightly colored bulletin board titled "Guess Who!" Have students guess the identities of the pictured babies and then lift the pages to check their answers.

Monkeying Around With Mammals

*There's no monkey business about it.
Students will enjoy this mammals lesson.*

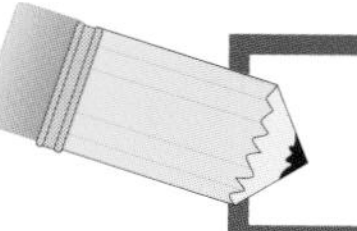

Skill: Identifying mammals

Estimated Lesson Time: 30 minutes

Teacher Preparation:

1. Draw two columns on a sheet of bulletin-board paper. Label one column "Mammals" and the other "Not Mammals."
2. For each student, write a different animal's name at the top of a sticky note. Be sure that most of the animals are mammals.
3. Duplicate a copy of page 29 for each student.

Materials:

1 labeled sticky note per student
1 copy of page 29 per student
bulletin-board paper
marker
crayons
chalk
chalkboard eraser

Background Information:

Characteristics of mammals

- Mammals have wool, fur, or hair on their bodies.
- Mammals have backbones and breathe with their lungs.
- Mammals are warm-blooded.
- Most mammals give birth to live young. Two mammals that do not give birth to live young are the spiny anteater and the duck-billed platypus.
- Baby mammals drink milk that is produced by their mother.

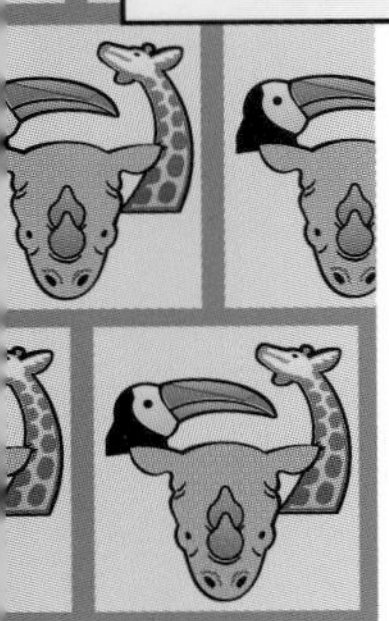

Introducing The Lesson:

Ask your students to name some of their favorite animals. Write students' responses on the chalkboard. Encourage students to explain what they like most about the animals they chose. After a short discussion, tell your students that they will be learning about *mammals* and their characteristics.

Steps:

1. Share with students the Background Information (page 27) about mammals' characteristics. Then revisit the students' list of their favorite animals. Ask student volunteers to erase from the list any animals that are not mammals.

2. Distribute a labeled sticky note to each student. Help students read the names of the animals on their notes. Then have each student use crayons to draw a picture of her animal on the sticky note. While students are drawing their animals, post the labeled bulletin-board paper in a prominent location.

3. Point out to students that the chart has a column for mammals and a column for animals that are not mammals. Have each student, in turn, attach her note under the appropriate column on the paper. Encourage each student to explain why she placed her note where she did.

4. Distribute a copy of page 29 to each student. Read the directions together, and have students complete the page independently.

5. Challenge students to complete the Bonus Box activity.

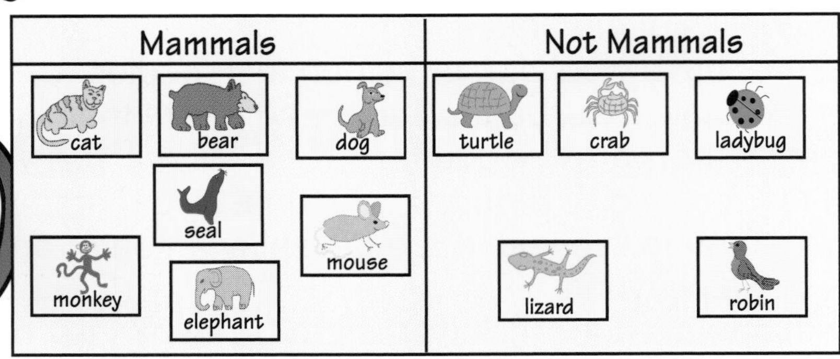

Name ______________________________ *Identifying mammals*

Are You A Mammal?

Write **yes** in the bubble if the animal is a *mammal*.
Write **no** in the bubble if the animal is *not a mammal*.
Color the mammals.

Bonus Box: On the back of this sheet, write the names of four more mammals. Draw a picture of each one.

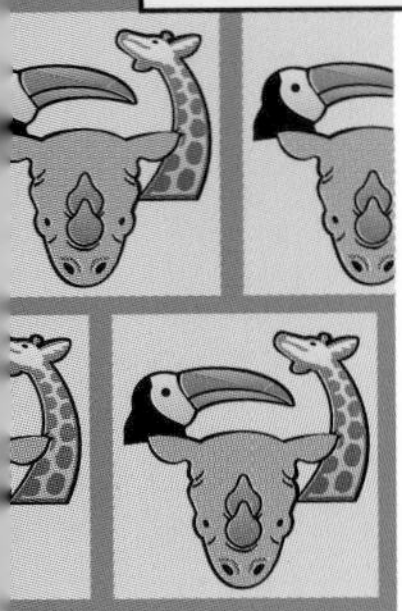

How To Extend The Lesson:

- Play the game Why Not? Divide students into small groups. Hold up a picture or photo of an animal that is not a mammal. Have a child from each group explain why the animal could not be a mammal. Continue playing until each player has had a turn.

- Share some of the following books about mammals:
  - — *Animals Born Alive And Well* by Ruth Heller (The Putnam Publishing Group, 1993)
  - — *Baby Whales Drink Milk* by Barbara Juster Esbensen (HarperCollins Children's Books, 1994)
  - — *About Mammals: A Guide For Children* by Cathryn Sill (Peachtree Publishers, Ltd.; 1997)

- Use this badge-making activity to remind students that humans are mammals. To make a badge, a student labels a three-inch construction-paper circle with a slogan such as "Proud To Be A Mammal!" Then he adds desired decorations and pins the badge to his shirt. Now that's mammal pride!

- Invite your students to research the different habitats in which animals live. Have students draw pictures of mammals or cut animal pictures from magazines. Mount these pictures on a bulletin board under headings labeled as shown. (If desired, add appropriate decorations to each strip.) Attach a short length of yarn from the top of each animal picture to its habitat; then add the title "Mammals Are Everywhere!"

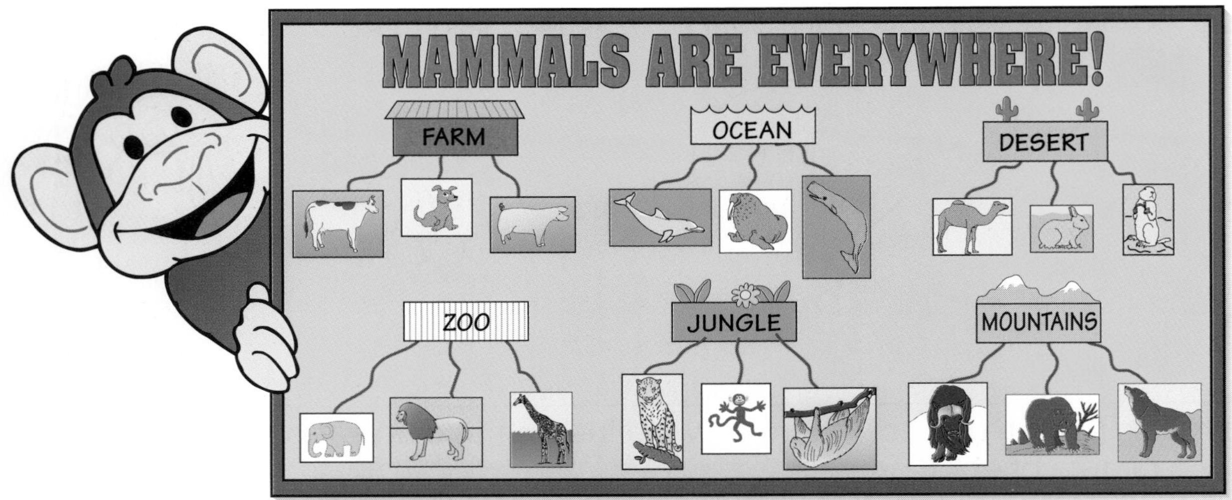

Inspecting Insects

Your classroom will be buzzing with enthusiasm over this insect lesson!

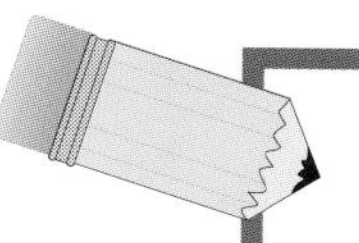

Skill: Identifying characteristics of insects

Estimated Lesson Time: 25 minutes

Teacher Preparation:

1. Draw an ant, a bee, and a butterfly on the chalkboard. Add the heading "Things That Are The Same." (See the illustrations on page 32.)
2. Duplicate page 33 for each student.

Materials:

1 copy of page 33 per student
1 paper clip per student
pencils
crayons

Background Information:

- Each insect has three body parts: *head, thorax,* and *abdomen.* The head is where an insect's eyes, antennae, and jaws are located. An insect's legs are attached to the thorax. Some insects have wings, which also are found on the thorax. The thorax and abdomen of some common insects may be hard to differentiate. Insects usually have six legs and may use their legs to run, walk, jump, dig, or sing. Insects do not have noses; they smell with their antennae.
- Spiders are closely related to insects, but do not belong to this species. In contrast to an insect, a spider has eight legs and only two main body parts—a *cephalothorax* and an abdomen. A spider does not have antennae or wings.

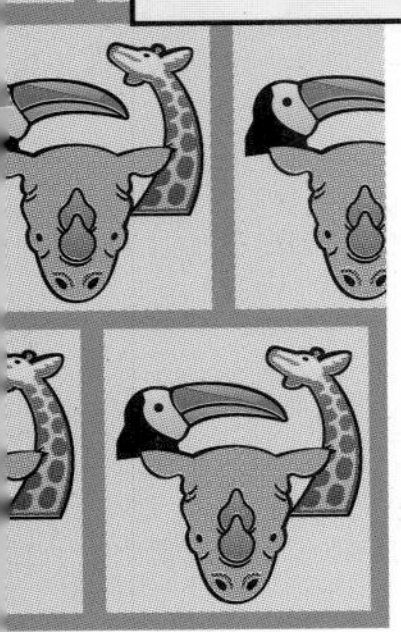

Introducing The Lesson:

Ask your students to study the drawings on the chalkboard. Challenge students to identify the characteristics that the pictured creatures have in common. List the named traits on the chalkboard. Explain that most insects have these characteristics. Then share the first item of Background Information on page 31.

Steps:

1. Draw a spider in a separate section of the chalkboard. Ask students to think about the characteristics listed on the chalkboard and to determine if spiders are also insects. Encourage students to explain their answers. Refer to the second item of Background Information on page 31, and explain that although spiders are often mistakenly thought of as insects, spiders do not belong to this species.

2. Tell students that they will play a game called Inspecting Insects. Distribute a copy of page 33 and a paper clip to each student. Divide students into pairs or groups of three. Demonstrate how to use the spinner on page 33 by placing a paper clip in the middle of the spinner. Then stand a pencil in the paper clip with one hand and spin the clip with your other hand.

3. To play the game, each student in turn spins and announces the space on which the spinner stops. He then colors the corresponding insect body part on his paper. (If the spinner lands on a leg, the student colors only one leg.) If the spinner lands on a section of the insect that has already been colored, the youngster loses his turn. The first player in each group to completely color his insect wins.

4. If desired, duplicate additional copies of the game for students to use at a center or to play at home.

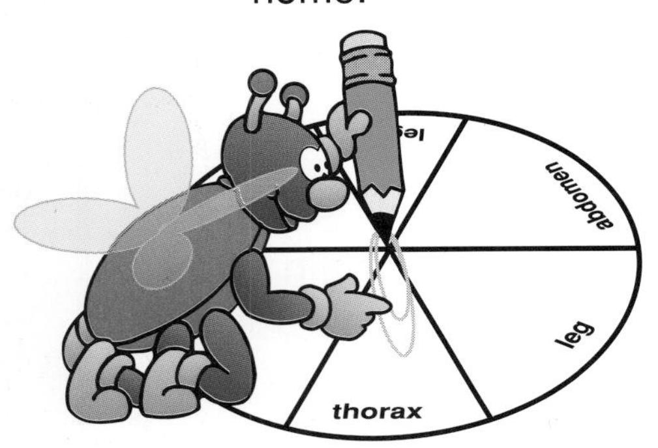

Identifying Insects

Play with one or two partners.
Take turns.
Use a paper clip and pencil to make a spinner.
Spin the paper clip.
Color.
The first player to color all of his or her insect wins!

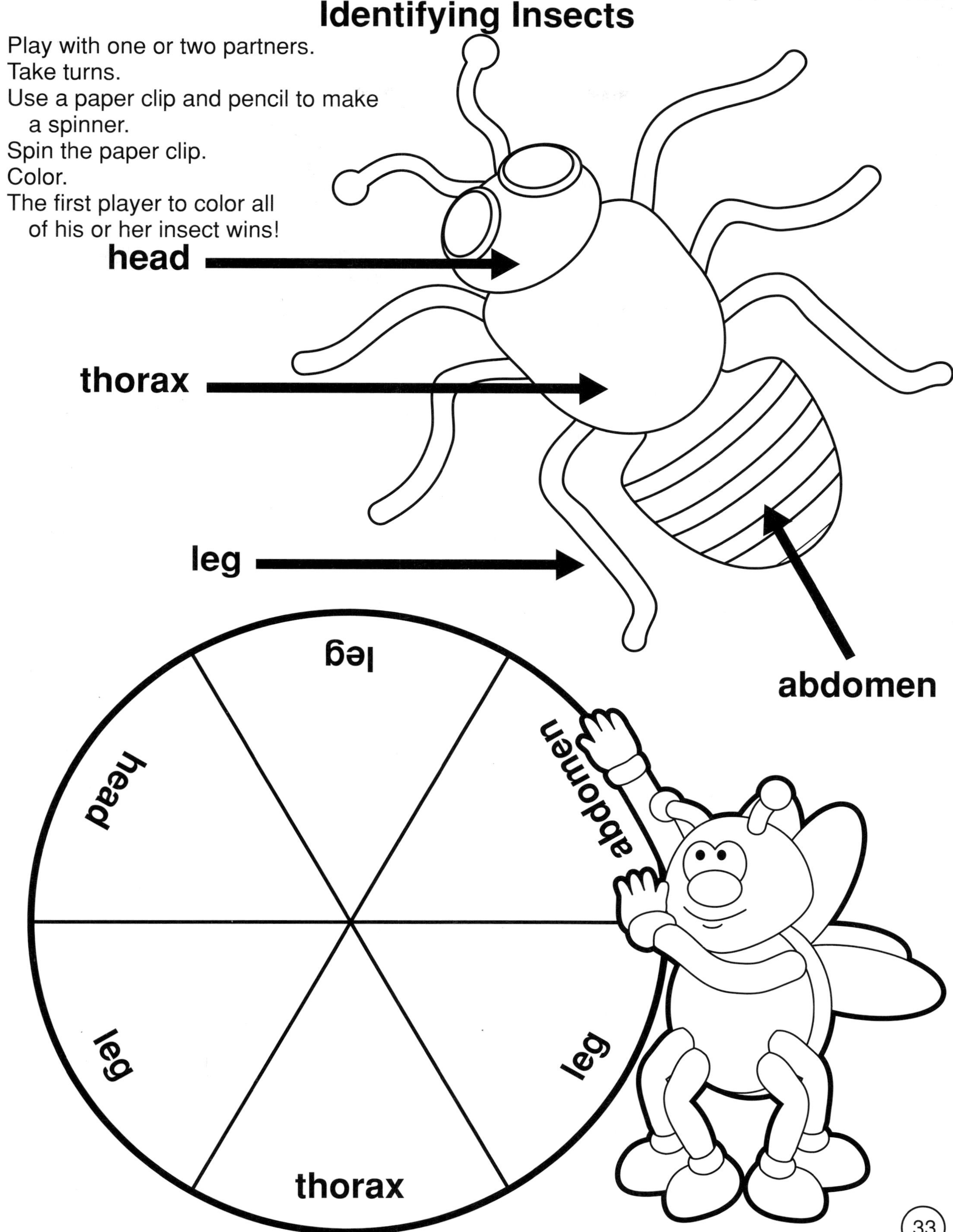

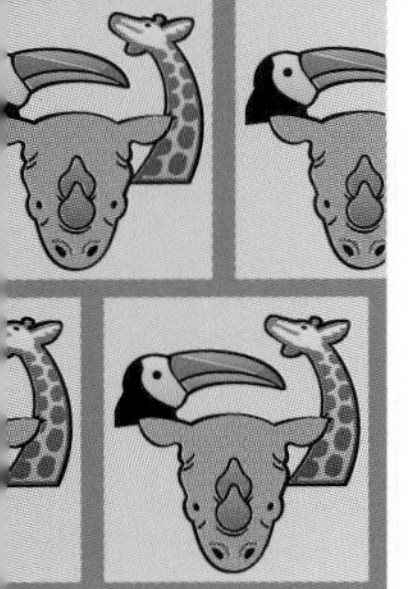

How To Extend The Lesson:

- Help students think about the world from an ant's perspective. First share the following information about ants:

  Ants are able to carry material that is heavier than their own weight. A square yard of soil may have thousands of ants. Many of the ants are not readily visible, though, because they are underground. Ants have different roles. The queen ant lays eggs. The nurse ants take care of the young ants. Soldier ants guard the colony. Worker ants build, search for food, and take care of the queen.

  Then read aloud *Two Bad Ants* by Chris Van Allsburg (Houghton Mifflin Company, 1988). This unique book describes the perilous experience two ants have when they can't resist the allure of a sugar bowl. After reading this story to your students, conduct a related shared writing activity. Enlist youngsters' help in writing and illustrating a story from an ant's point of view. Compile and bind the pages with a cover; then add the completed book to your classroom library.

- Have students demonstrate their knowledge about the characteristics of insects with this project. First review the distinguishing features of insects. Then give each student a portion of clay. Instruct each child to make a clay insect. Each youngster can model his insect to look like an actual insect or use his imagination to create his own, as long as the clay figure has the characteristics of an insect. After each student has completed his model, have him place the insect on a sheet of paper. Then have him label each insect part near the corresponding part of his model.

- Integrate math and science with this nifty idea! Remind students that each insect has six legs and a head, a thorax, and an abdomen. Create insect word problems like the ones shown. Encourage youngsters to show their answers with pictures and words. Provide an opportunity for students to make similar word problems for their classmates.

Build-A-Bird!

Give your students something to crow about with this fun activity about birds!

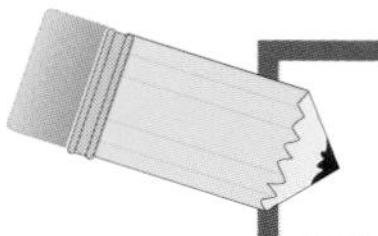

Skill: Identifying characteristics of birds

Estimated Lesson Time: 45 minutes

Teacher Preparation:

1. Draw a bird body on the chalkboard similar to the one shown.
2. Duplicate and cut out one set of the cards on page 37.
3. Duplicate page 37 for each student.

Materials:

1 copy of page 37 for teacher use
1 copy of page 37 per student
1 sheet of drawing paper per student
scissors
chalk

Background Information:

- A bird is a warm-blooded animal that has a backbone, feathers, wings, and two legs, and breathes through lungs.
- There are more than 9,700 living species of birds in the world.
- Birds are found all over the world and in all types of climates.
- Feathers help keep birds warm. They also aid in flight and steering. Although all birds have wings, not all birds can fly. (The ostrich and penguin, for example, are flightless.)
- Birds' beaks are adapted to the food they eat.
- Birds, as a class, have the best vision of all animals.
- All birds hatch from eggs. Most birds build nests to lay their eggs in.
- The smallest living bird is the *bee hummingbird*, which grows to only about two inches long.
- The largest living bird is the *ostrich,* which may grow up to eight feet tall.

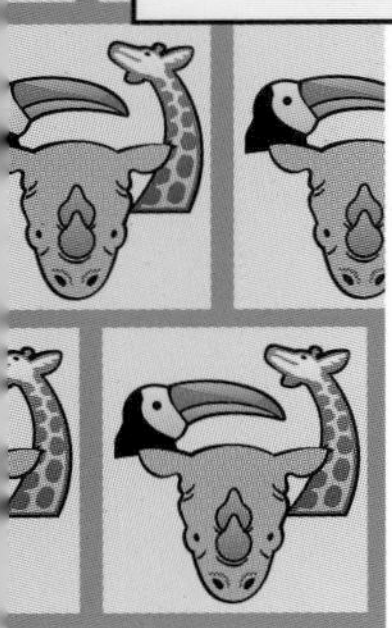

Introducing The Lesson:

Have students name several characteristics of birds. List students' responses on the chalkboard. Then tell students that they will play a game that will help them review the characteristics of a bird.

Steps:

1. Share the Background Information about birds on page 35. Add desired information to the student-generated list of characteristics on the chalkboard.

2. Use the chalkboard drawing and the precut cards from page 37 as you explain the following rules for the game Build-A-Bird!

   Directions for playing Build-A-Bird!:
   - The game is for two players.
   - Each player needs a set of the cards from page 37, a sheet of drawing paper, and a pencil.
   - Each player shuffles his cards and places them facedown in front of him.
   - Player 1 turns over his top card. If the card is part of a bird, he draws the part on his bird body. If it is not part of a bird, the player places the card in a discard pile, and it is Player 2's turn.
   - Player 2 turns over his top card and takes his turn as did Player 1.
   - Play continues until one player's bird is complete with two eyes, a beak, feathers, wings, a tail, and two legs.

3. Distribute one copy of page 37 and one sheet of drawing paper to each student. Instruct the students to cut out the cards on their pages, then draw a bird body on their papers that is similar to the one on the chalkboard.

4. Pair students; then have them follow the rules to play Build-A-Bird!

Name ____________________

Build-A-Bird!

Follow your teacher's directions to play this game.

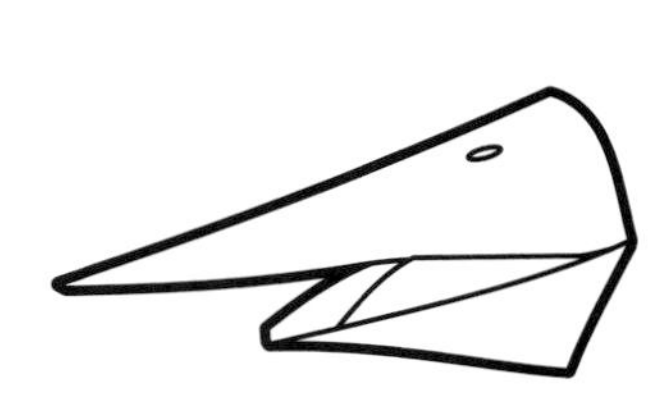 **beak**	 **feathers**	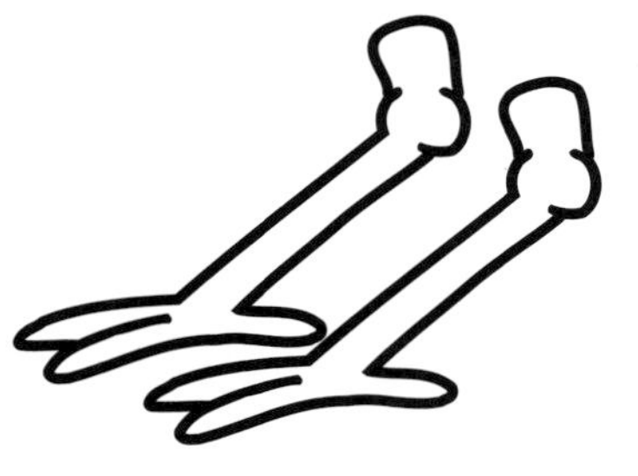 **two legs**
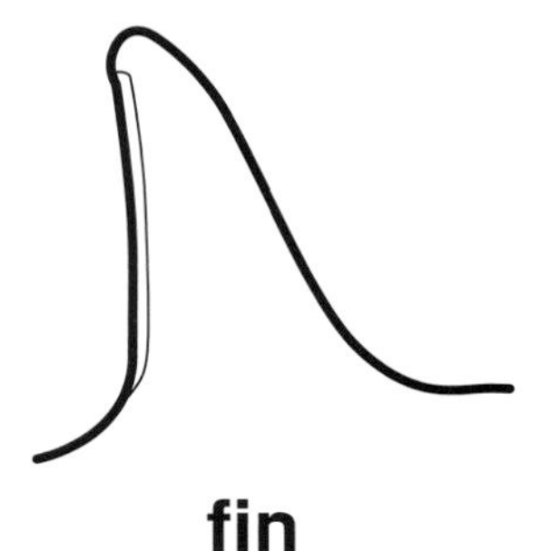 **fin**	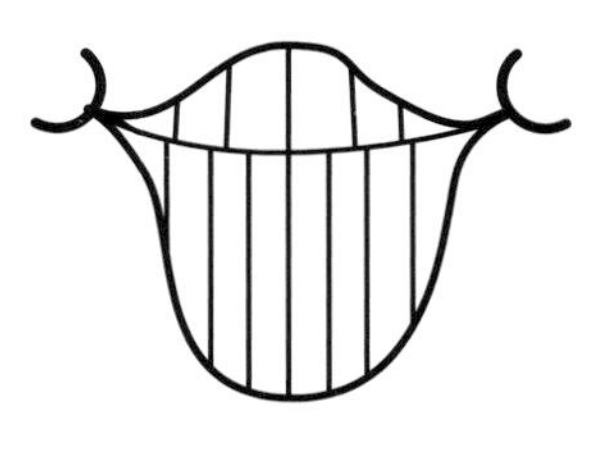 **teeth**	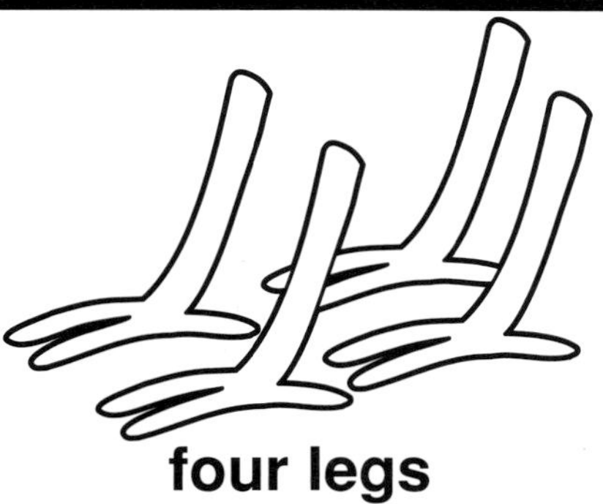 **four legs**
two wings	 **antennae**	 **whiskers**
 **a tail**	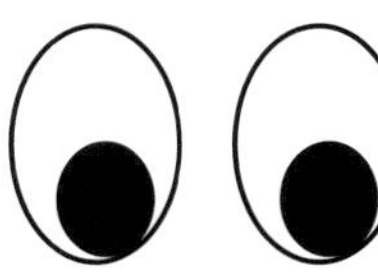 **two eyes**	 **hair**

How To Extend The Lesson:

- Create this unique reading center to display your books about birds. Fill a large brown basket with long brown construction-paper strips. Place some of your favorite books about birds in the resulting nest, and store the nest of books at your classroom library. Some good choices of bird books are:
  - — *About Birds* by Cathryn Sill (Peachtree Publishers, Ltd.; 1997)
  - — *What Makes A Bird A Bird?* by May Garelick (Mondo Publishing, 1995)
  - — *Have You Seen Birds?* by Joanne Oppenheim (Scholastic Inc., 1988)
  - — *Bird* (Eyewitness Books) by David Burnie (Alfred A. Knopf Books For Young Readers, 1988)

- Students will test their wings with this activity! Have students flap their arms for approximately one minute. Ask students how their arms feel. Then remind students that a bird's wings wouldn't be tired, because their wings are adapted for flapping. Therefore birds can flap their wings for long periods of time. Some birds combine flapping flight with gliding or soaring, both of which require little energy. After sharing this information, tell students that some birds flap their wings faster than other birds. For example a crow's wings beat 20 times in 10 seconds, but a chickadee's wings beat 270 times every 10 seconds. Pair students and encourage each student (in turn) to try flapping his arms as fast as he can for ten seconds while his partner times him. Do you have any fast flappers in your classroom?

- Students will love eating these edible nests! In advance melt one 12-ounce bag of butterscotch chips over low heat. Add two 3-ounce cans of chow-mein noodles, and stir until the noodles are well coated. Spread the mixture out on a cookie sheet until cooled; then place in a resealable plastic bag until ready for use. On the day of the lesson, provide students with the nest mixture, plastic knives, chocolate frosting, jelly beans, and plain doughnuts. Have each student use a plastic knife to spread chocolate icing atop his doughnut and then sprinkle on the nest mixture. For a finishing touch, have each youngster place two or three jelly beans in his nest.

Spin A Season!

Put your students in a sunny mood with this interactive activity that reinforces season recognition.

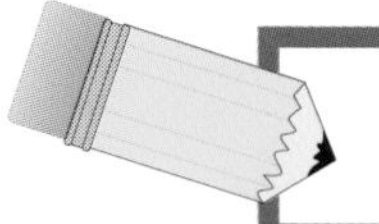

Skill: Recognizing attributes of seasons

Estimated Lesson Time: 30 minutes

Teacher Preparation:

Duplicate page 41 onto white construction paper for each student.

Materials:

1 white construction-paper copy of page 41 per student
1 brad per student
crayons
scissors

Background Information:

- The Earth's revolution around the Sun causes the different seasons.
- When it is summer in the Northern Hemisphere, it is winter in the Southern Hemisphere.
- Places near the polar regions have light and dark seasons. The Sun shines almost all the time in the summer and hardly ever in the winter.
- In ancient times people used to celebrate the first day of spring because it was the beginning of the growing season.
- The shortest day of the year occurs on the first day of winter.
- The longest day of the year occurs on the first day of summer.
- Places near the equator have only dry and rainy periods. The seasons do not really change a whole lot.

Introducing The Lesson:

Ask students to look outside and describe the current season. Create a list on the chalkboard of students' observations about the weather, vegetation, and clothing being worn.

Steps:

1. Distribute a copy of page 41 to each student. Instruct students to color the seasonal pictures on the circle.

2. Have students cut out the circle and the spinner.

3. Assist each student in using the brad to attach the spinner to the circle.

4. Read the following review questions aloud to your students. After each question, have students point their spinners to the season that depicts their answers. Then direct students to hold their spinners up to reveal their answers. Quickly verify students' responses, discussing discrepancies as needed. If desired encourage students to create their own questions for their classmates to answer.

Review Questions:

- In what season does it snow the most? *(winter)*
- In what season are seeds usually planted? *(spring)*
- In what season do leaves fall from trees? *(fall)*
- In what season are many baby animals born? *(spring)*
- In what season is the temperature the hottest? *(summer)*
- In what season is the month of May? *(spring)*
- In what season do leaves change colors? *(fall)*
- In what season do we celebrate the Fourth of July? *(summer)*
- In what season are heavy coats, hats, and mittens worn? *(winter)*
- In what season are swimsuits, sandals, and tank tops worn? *(summer)*
- In what season do some animals hibernate? *(winter)*
- In what season do some birds migrate south? *(fall)*

Name ________________________________ *Recognizing attributes of seasons*

Spin A Season!

Color.
Cut.
Follow your teacher's directions.

How To Extend The Lesson:

- Challenge students to create seasonal collages. To make a collage, each youngster chooses a season and writes a list of items that correspond to his season. (For example a student choosing winter might list items such as snow, Christmas, hearts, winter clothing, and bare trees.) For each item on his list, he draws a picture of it or finds a picture of it in a magazine. Then he glues the pictures to a sheet of construction paper. After students complete their collages, post them on a bulletin board titled "Name The Season." Encourage students to guess what season is represented on each collage.

- Create a seasonal classification center. To create the center, place seasonal pictures of objects—such as leaves, swimsuits, snowmen, sunglasses, and sweatshirts—at a table. Label an index card for each season. Have student pairs work together to sort and classify the pictures into the correct seasons.

- Share the story *The Berenstain Bears' Four Seasons Storybook* by Stan and Jan Berenstain (Random House Books For Young Readers, 1996). Have students describe the different bear activities during each of the four seasons. Then have each child fold a sheet of white construction paper to create four equal boxes. Have the child unfold his paper, then label the top of each section with the name of a different season. Finally instruct each student to illustrate and label a bear activity for each season.

- Use this activity to combine poetry with your study of the seasons. To begin review what an acrostic poem is with your students. Then have each child select a season and write its name vertically down the left side of a sheet of paper. Instruct students to write a word or phrase to correspond with each letter of the season's name. If desired have students illustrate their seasonal poems.

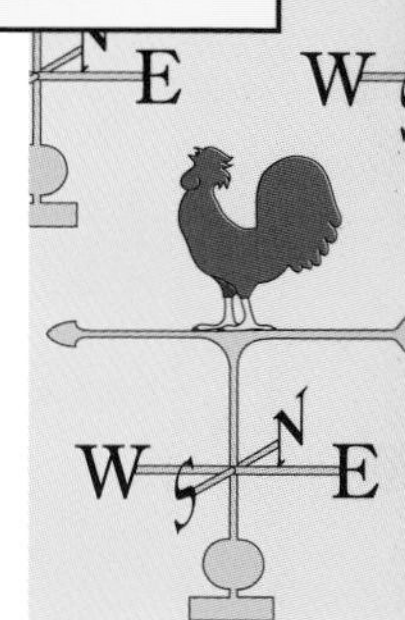

Clouds! Clouds! Clouds!

Have some fun exploring the fantastic formations of clouds with your students!

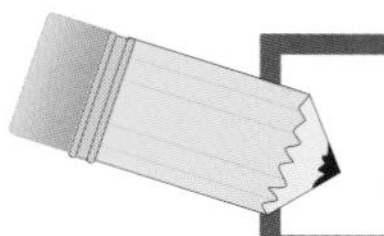

Skill: Identifying cloud types (stratus, cirrus, cumulus, cumulonimbus)

Estimated Lesson Time: 40 minutes

Teacher Preparation:

1. Draw or find pictures of the four cloud types featured in this lesson. Be sure that each cloud picture is on a different piece of paper and large enough for all students to view at once.
2. Write each of the four cloud types on its own sentence strip.
3. Place one teaspoon of black or gray powdered tempera paint into a bag of cotton balls. Shake until well mixed.
4. Duplicate page 45 for each student.

Materials:

1 cloud drawing or picture of each of the four featured clouds
1 teaspoon of black or gray powdered tempera paint
one 12" x 18" sheet of blue construction paper per student
4 sentence-strip cloud labels
3 bags of cotton balls
1 copy of page 45 per student
glue
scissors

Background Information:

- Clouds are masses of water droplets or ice crystals that float in the air.
- Most clouds change shape continually.
- There are three main types of clouds: *cirrus, cumulus,* and *stratus.*
- Scientists give names to clouds that describe their appearance.
  - —*Strato-* means layerlike or sheetlike. Stratus clouds appear as layers or sheets.
  - —*Cumulo-* means pile or heap. Cumulus clouds are piled-up masses of white clouds.
  - —*Cirro-* means curl. Cirrus clouds are curly white clouds.

  These terms and a few others are used to form the names of the most common clouds.
- Clouds are grouped into different classes according to their height above the ground.

Introducing The Lesson:

Take your youngsters outside and ask them to look at the clouds. Encourage students to describe any shapes or objects made by the clouds. (If this activity is not possible due to the weather, ask students to close their eyes and imagine several clouds in the sky.) Then tell students that they will be studying and making their own clouds today.

Steps:

1. Display the four cloud pictures. Show students the sentence strip labeled "Cirrus Clouds." Then read the following description: *"Cirrus* clouds are the highest clouds in the sky. They look like white, feathery streaks and can be seen on fair-weather days." Call on a student volunteer to choose the cloud picture that matches the description.

2. Use the following descriptions to repeat this activity with the remaining three cloud types:
   - *Stratus* clouds are the lowest clouds. They look like a blanket of gray in the sky. Stratus clouds may bring light rain or snow.
   - *Cumulus* clouds are the puffy, white clouds that we often see on bright, sunny days. These clouds change their shapes often.
   - *Cumulonimbus* clouds, also called thunderheads, look like cumulus clouds because they are large and puffy. However, these clouds are gray or black and usually bring heavy storms.

3. Distribute a copy of page 45, one sheet of white construction paper, and a handful of gray cotton balls and white cotton balls to each student.

4. Have each student write her name on the heading. Next instruct her to cut out the heading and the labels on the reproducible and glue them to the construction paper as shown. Then read each description of the cloud types. For each label, the student shapes the appropriately colored cotton balls to depict the specified cloud and glues them above the label.

Clouds

by ________________________

Stratus Clouds
Stratus clouds look like a blanket of gray in the sky.
These low clouds may bring light rain or snow.

Cirrus Clouds
Cirrus clouds are very high in the sky. They look like white, feathery streaks and are usually seen on fair-weather days.

Cumulus Clouds
Cumulus clouds are the puffy, white clouds that are often seen on bright, sunny days.

Cumulonimbus Clouds
Cumulonimbus clouds are also called thunderheads.
These puffy, dark clouds bring heavy storms.

How To Extend The Lesson:

- No cloud lesson would be complete without reading *It Looked Like Spilt Milk* by Charles G. Shaw (HarperCollins Publishers, Inc.; 1988). In advance program one sheet of light blue construction paper for every student with the sentence "My ________ is really just a cloud in the sky!" Then, after sharing this classic cloud tale with your students, give each student one sheet of the blue construction paper and a handful of white cotton balls. Instruct him to glue the cotton to create an object that he imagines may appear in the clouds. Then have the child write the name of the object on the line provided. Invite students to share their pictures with their classmates.

- Have your students keep a daily log of the types of clouds they see in the sky. Each morning select a different student to record the observed cloud type. At the end of the month, enlist students' help to tally the occurrence of each cloud type and then to create a graph depicting the results.

- Share some of the following cloud stories with your students:
  —*The Cloud Book* by Tomie dePaola (Holiday House, Inc.; 1984)
  —*Cloud Nine* by Norman Silver (Clarion Books, 1995)
  —*Little Cloud* by Eric Carle (Philomel Books, 1996)

- Your youngsters will enjoy making these picture-perfect, cloudy-day creations. Each child will need one 9" x 12" sheet of light blue construction paper, three 9-inch strips of black construction paper, three 12-inch strips of black construction paper, a supply of scrap paper in a variety of colors, scissors, and glue. To make a cloudy-day window scene, a child chooses a cloud type and uses the paper scraps to create those clouds. He glues the clouds to the blue paper and then adds an accompanying scene. Finally he glues the paper strips atop the scene to create a windowlike frame as shown.

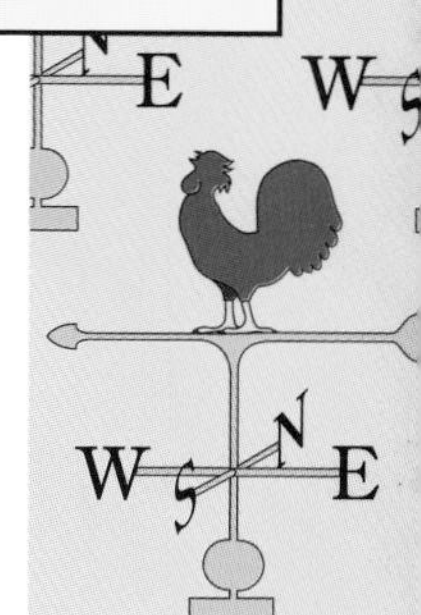

Learning By Degrees

Youngsters will warm up to reading thermometers with this interactive weather lesson.

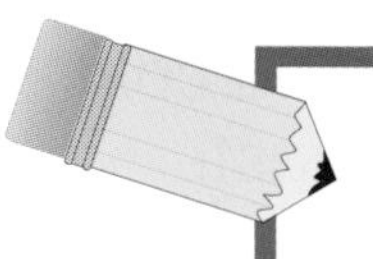

Skill: Reading and interpreting thermometers

Estimated Lesson Time: 30 minutes

Teacher Preparation:

1. Draw three columns on the chalkboard. Label the columns "Hot," "Warm," and "Cold."
2. Duplicate page 49 for each student.

Materials:

1 cup of ice water
1 thermometer
1 paper towel
1 copy of page 49 per student
paper towels
scissors
glue

Background Information:

- Gabriel Daniel Fahrenheit (1686–1736) developed the Fahrenheit temperature scale. His idea to use mercury in thermometers, rather than alcohol and water, increased the accuracy of thermometer readings. Fahrenheit determined these fixed temperatures: 0° for the freezing point of ice, salt, and water; 32° for the freezing point of pure water; and 212° for the boiling point of water.

- Liquid-in-glass thermometers are commonly used for cooking, taking body temperature, and for many other daily functions. Mercury is the most frequently used liquid for this type of thermometer. When the temperature of mercury increases, the mercury expands and rises up the thermometer tube. When the mercury cools, it contracts and moves down the tube.

Introducing The Lesson:

Have students brainstorm activities and clothing that are suitable for hot weather. Record youngsters' answers on the chalkboard under the appropriate heading. Then repeat this exercise with the categories of warm and cold weather. Explain that this lesson will teach youngsters how to use a thermometer to determine if the temperature is hot, warm, or cold.

Steps:

1. Gather students around as you hold the bulb of the thermometer in your hands for a few minutes. Ask students to look at the mercury level of the thermometer. Then place the thermometer in the water. Ask students to observe the thermometer and to note any changes. After a few minutes, ask student volunteers to share their observations. Then empty the cup and dry the thermometer with the provided paper towels.

2. Share the Background Information on page 47. Explain how to use the thermometer scale, and provide an opportunity for students to practice reading thermometers.

3. Distribute a copy of page 49 to each student. Have him write the temperature shown on the blank below each thermometer. Then have him cut out the pictures at the bottom of his page and glue them below the appropriate thermometers.

Name ______________________________

Learning By Degrees

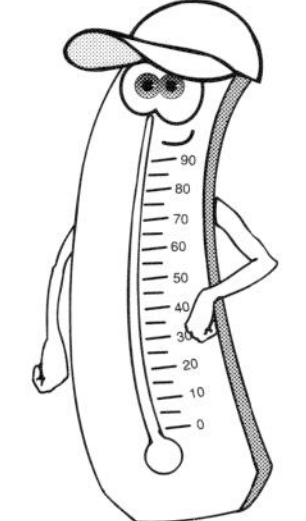

Read the thermometers.
Write the temperatures.
Cut out the pictures.
Glue them in the correct columns.

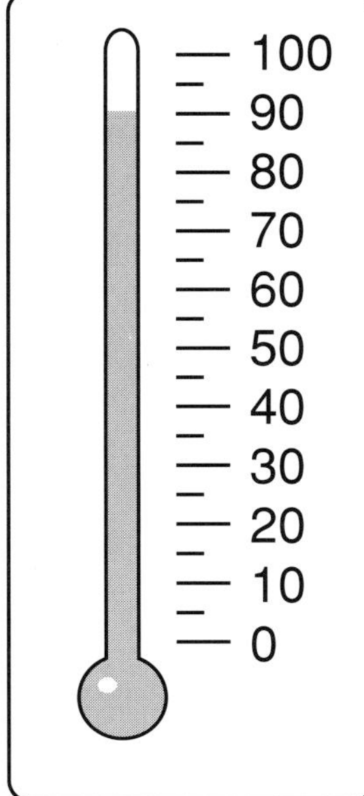

Hot

____

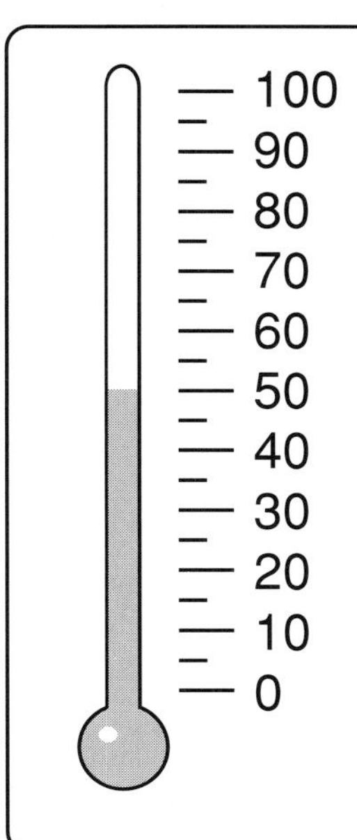

Warm

____

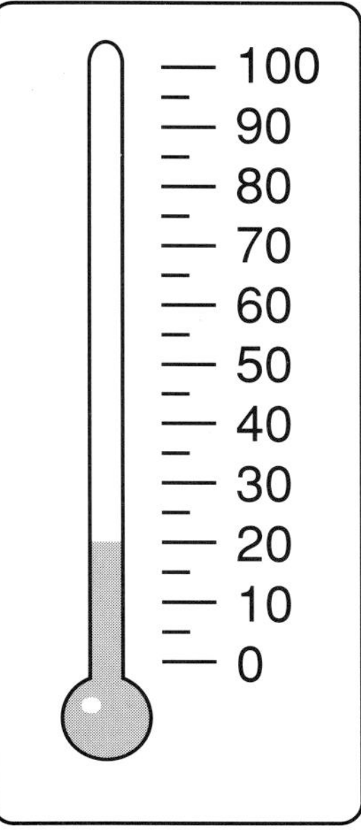

Cold

____

How To Extend The Lesson:

- Ask each youngster to bring an article of clothing to school. Be sure to have a few extra pieces of clothing available for students who do not bring any. Tell students that they are going to play a temperature and clothing matching game. To prepare draw three simple thermometers on the chalkboard, each indicating a different temperature: cold, warm, and hot. Label each thermometer. Also have each youngster write his name on a piece of masking tape and attach it to his article of clothing. To begin the game, point to one of the thermometers and ask students to stand if they have clothing that is appropriate for that temperature. After quickly verifying students' responses, repeat the activity with the other thermometers. If desired have each student trade his article of clothing with a classmate and continue play.

- Conduct a science experiment with thermometers. Place one thermometer on a sheet of white paper and another thermometer on a sheet of black paper. Instruct students to read each thermometer. Place the thermometers outside in a sunny place. After a period of time, have students read their thermometers. Lead students in a discussion about their observations and how the results relate to wardrobe choices.

- Introduce youngsters to hyperboles with this writing activity. Help each student write a sentence exaggerating about a time when it was hot or cold. Write each student's sentence on a separate sheet of paper and have him illustrate it. Write the title "The Day The Temperature Was Out Of Control" on another sheet of paper, and decorate it as desired to make a cover. Bind the completed pages with the cover to create a unique addition to your classroom library.

It was so cold that my little brother turned into an ice cube.

Presenting Precipitation!

The forecast calls for weather-wise students with this classification activity.

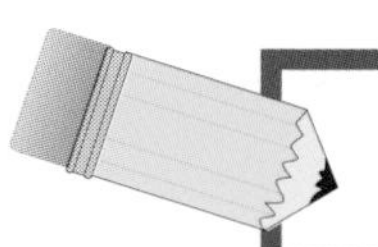

Skill: Identifying types of precipitation

Estimated Lesson Time: 30 minutes

Teacher Preparation:

1. Enlarge and duplicate one set of the weather cards on page 53 (excluding the sun, cloud, and rainbow cards).
2. Duplicate page 53 for each student.

Materials:

1 copy of page 53 per student
scissors
glue

Background Information:

Precipitation is any type of rain or snow. The types of precipitation presented in this lesson are described below.

Rain: When water evaporates, the resulting water vapor rises and cools. The water vapor condenses into water droplets, and the water droplets create clouds. When the water droplets become too big for the air to carry them, they fall as rain.
Snow: Snow begins to form when water vapor turns to ice crystals. When the crystals cling together, they create snowflakes. Snowflakes each have six sides, and no two snowflakes are alike.
Drizzle: Drizzle drops are one-fifth the size of the smallest raindrop. Drizzle occurs when warm, damp air comes in contact with colder air or ground temperatures.
Hail: Hail is frozen precipitation that is produced by thunderstorms. Hailstones are formed when ice crystals are blown up into colder air and a layer of ice forms around them. The ice crystals are taken back up into the cold air again and again, creating additional layers of ice. When the ice crystals become too heavy for the air to hold them any longer, they fall to the ground as hailstones. If you cut a hailstone in half, you will see a ring for each layer.
Sleet: Sleet is partly melted snow or a mixture of snow and rain.

Introducing The Lesson:

Ask students to brainstorm different types of precipitation. Then discuss with youngsters how precipitation affects our lives. For example, snow influences our clothing choices, and rain helps our plants and gardens grow.

Steps:

1. Use the Background Information on page 51 to define the word precipitation and tell students how rain, snow, drizzle, hail, and sleet are formed.

2. Explain that precipitation affects our lives in both a positive and negative manner. For example, rain supplies plants with water, but hail may damage cars and homes.

3. Show students an enlarged weather card. Have youngsters identify the type of precipitation shown and name either a positive or negative effect that it has on our lives. Continue with the remaining cards in a similar manner.

4. Distribute page 53 to students. Have each child cut out the pictures on his sheet. Then instruct students to identify each of the pictured items and determine whether or not it is a type of precipitation. Direct youngsters to glue each picture under the appropriate umbrella.

5. Challenge students to complete the Bonus Box activity.

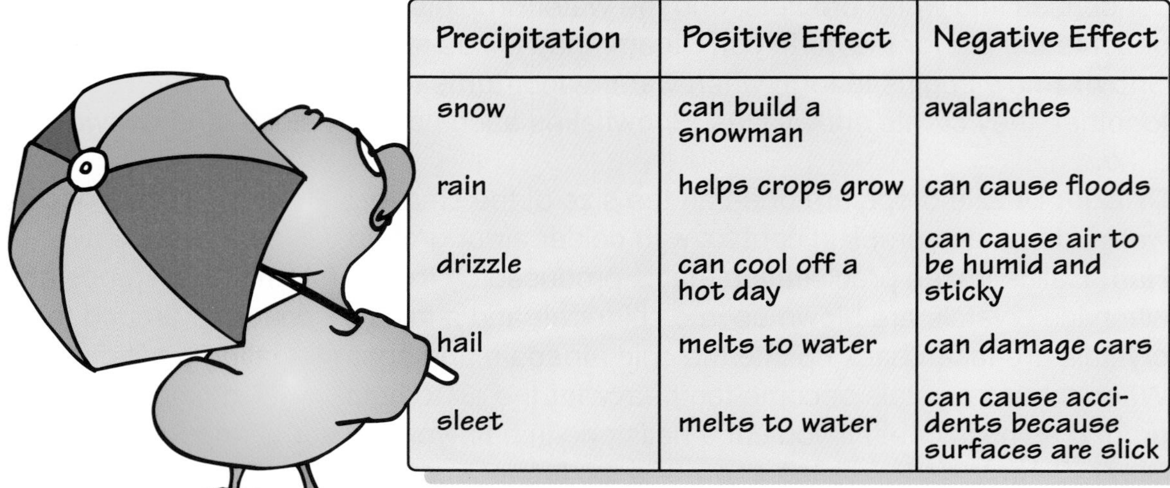

Precipitation	Positive Effect	Negative Effect
snow	can build a snowman	avalanches
rain	helps crops grow	can cause floods
drizzle	can cool off a hot day	can cause air to be humid and sticky
hail	melts to water	can damage cars
sleet	melts to water	can cause accidents because surfaces are slick

Name ______________________ *Identifying types of precipitation*

Presenting Precipitation

Cut out the pictures.
Glue the precipitation pictures under the new umbrella.
Glue the other pictures under the old umbrella.

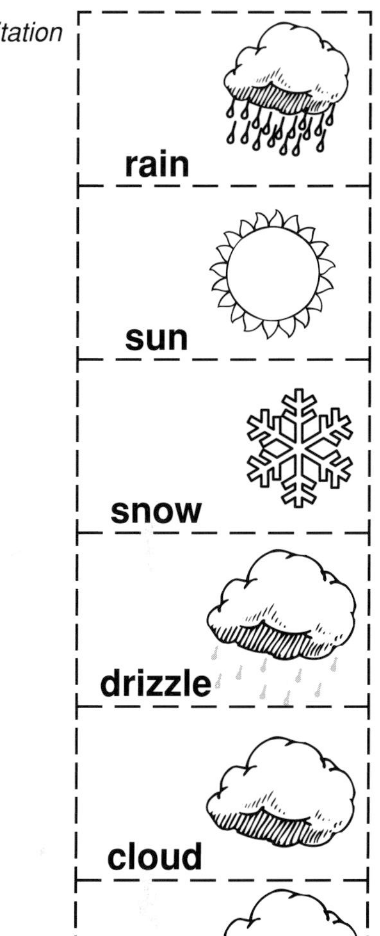

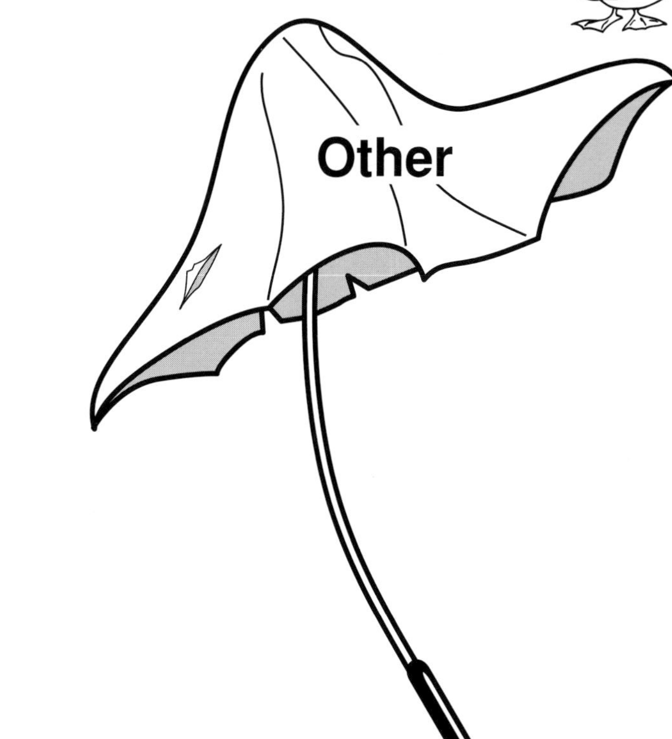

Bonus Box: On the back of this sheet, write a sentence describing your favorite type of precipitation.

How To Extend The Lesson:

- Make a rain gauge with your students. You will need one empty two-liter plastic bottle, scissors or a knife, a permanent marker, a wooden stake, several large rubber bands, and a hammer. To make the rain gauge, remove the top third of the bottle; then invert the top inside the bottom of the bottle, forming a funnel. Use the marker to make a desired scale on the side of the bottle. With a hammer, drive the stake into level ground in an open area of your schoolyard. Set the bottle beside the stake. Use rubber bands to secure the bottle to the stake. Then enlist students' help in taking daily readings of the rainfall amount. Record the rainfall amount on a classroom graph. Each time you record a measurement, pour out the rainwater that was collected in the bottle.

- Read aloud *Cloudy With A Chance Of Meatballs* written by Judi Barrett and illustrated by Ron Barrett (Simon & Schuster Children's Division, 1982). Then have students use this book as a model to write their own creative stories, such as "The Day It Rained Cats And Dogs" or "The Time It Rained Money."

- Make a toy microphone by molding a ball of aluminum foil around the top of a cardboard tube or wooden dowel. Each day select a student to use the microphone to announce the weather.

- For a webbing activity, ask each youngster to select a type of precipitation. Direct him to write the chosen precipitation in the center of a large sheet of paper. Have the child brainstorm positive and negative effects of this type of precipitation, and instruct him to outline his ideas in a web.

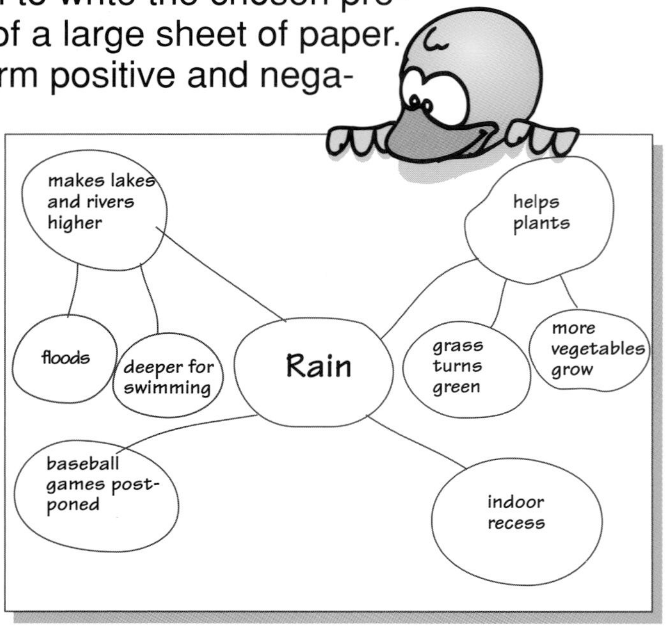

The Conscientious Recycling Crew

Teach students the importance of protecting our planet with this constructive lesson!

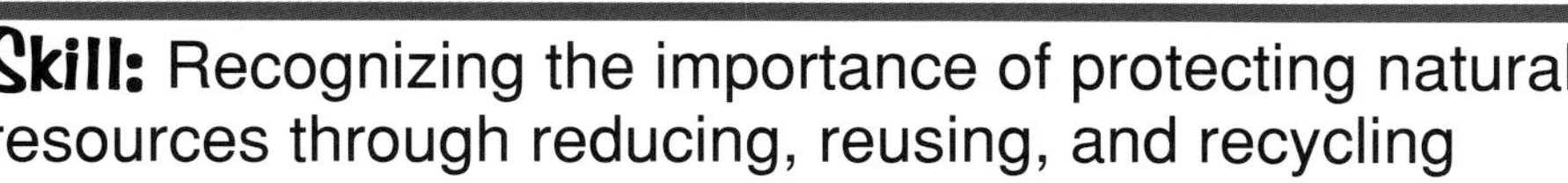

Skill: Recognizing the importance of protecting natural resources through reducing, reusing, and recycling

Estimated Lesson Time: 30 minutes

Teacher Preparation:

1. Duplicate page 57 for each student.
2. Cut out a magazine picture of each of the following items (or draw and label each item on a separate index card): an old T-shirt, a glass jar, an aluminum pie pan, a plastic bottle, and a cardboard milk container.

Materials:

1 copy of page 57 per student
a book in fairly poor condition, but still readable
5 different magazine pictures (or labeled index cards)

Background Information:

Producing some of the products we use at home and at school takes materials from the environment, uses energy, and causes pollution. Therefore the more we throw away, the more we harm the environment. *Reducing, reusing,* and *recycling* helps minimize these problems.

- **Reducing** means lessening the amount of trash through wise buying of items with little packaging. Styrofoam® is one item that we should try to buy less of since it is not biodegradable and causes problems in landfills.
- **Reusing** means not discarding items after one use; items are used again for the same function or a different function. Grocery bags are items that can be reused. After you unpack the groceries, the bags can be saved and used on your next trip to the store. Or they can be used to line trash cans.
- **Recycling** is the process of turning used materials into new products. Aluminum cans are recycled to make new cans.

Introducing The Lesson:

Walk over to the trash can and throw away the book. Since students are sure to be surprised by your actions, ask them why they are surprised. Then encourage them to share ideas about what could be done with the book instead of throwing it away. Lead students to the conclusion that we can *reduce, reuse,* and *recycle* unwanted materials.

Steps:

1. Tell students that the principal has appointed them members of the Conscientious Recycling Crew. To retain their membership, they must learn more about protecting the planet. Share with students the Background Information on page 55.

2. In turn display each picture card and have students provide examples—such as those below—of how items can be reduced, reused, or recycled.

3. Remind students that Earth needs their help, and as members of the Conscientious Recycling Crew, the best way they can help is to reduce, reuse, and recycle. Next give each student a copy of the Protect-The-Planet Pledge on page 57. Read the pledge with students. Then have each student write her name on the top line and list three conservation measures she can perform at home and three measures she can perform at school. Finally have her sign her name and write the date on the provided lines.

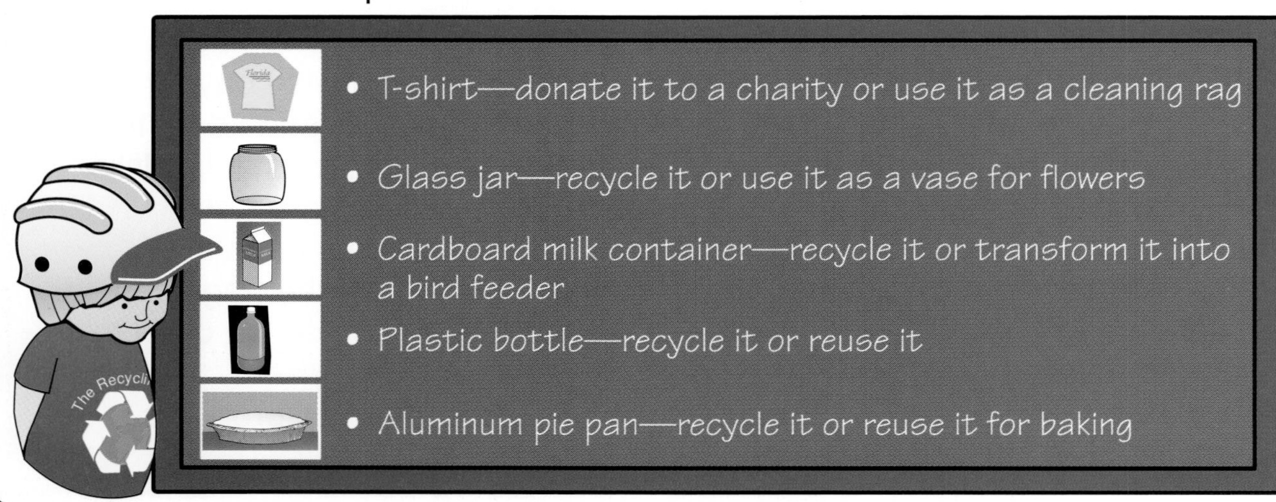

Thanks for your help!

Protect-The-Planet Pledge

I, ______________________________, promise to do my best to
(your name)

reduce, reuse, and recycle unwanted materials.

Here is a list of the things I plan to do:

At Home:

1.

2.

3.

At School:

1.

2.

3.

Recycling crew member: ______________________________
(signature)

Date: ______________________

How To Extend The Lesson:

- Have students create recycling puzzles. Have each student write and illustrate an idea for taking care of Earth on an eight-inch tagboard circle. Then have each student flip her resulting project to its blank side and draw a predetermined number of puzzle pieces. Next have her cut the project on the lines and place the puzzle pieces in a resealable plastic bag. Encourage students to put together their own and their classmates' puzzles in their free time.

- Demonstrate recycling firsthand with this nifty idea. Have students peel the labels from small or broken crayons, then sort them by color. Place crayons of the same color in a microwave-safe dish. Microwave on low, stirring occasionally. Then pour the melted crayon wax into candy molds. Place the molds in the freezer; then pop out the crayon shapes when solid. No doubt students will enjoy coloring with these cool crayon creations!

- Take the Protect-The-Planet Pledge from page 57 one step further with the help of contracts. To begin create a contract that lists several planet-protecting tasks that students included on their pledge sheets. Also consider these tasks: turning off the lights each time you leave a room; carrying your lunch to school in a lunchbox rather than a paper bag; donating old toys, books, and clothing to a charity; and sorting your family's garbage for recycling. Beside each task draw a small box. Give each student a copy of the contract and instruct him to check each box as he completes the activity. Present each student who completes a predetermined number of tasks with a personalized copy of the award shown below.

Award

Friends Of The Earth Award

presented to

Conscientious Recycling Crew Member

____
(student)

______________________________ ______________
(teacher's signature) (date)

Far-Out Facts

Blast into space with this "sun-sational" booklet-making activity!

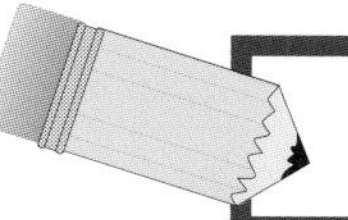

Skill: Learning about the Sun and the Moon

Estimated Lesson Time: 30 minutes

Teacher Preparation:

1. Write "Sun" on one large index card, "Moon" on another index card, and "Earth" on a third card.
2. Divide a sheet of chart paper into two columns. Label one column "Sun" and the other column "Moon."
3. Duplicate page 61 for each student.

Materials:

1 sheet of labeled chart paper
3 large labeled index cards
1 copy of page 61 per student
scissors
stapler
crayons

Background Information:

The Sun: The Sun, the closest star to Earth, is at the center of the solar system. The Sun's diameter is approximately 865,000 miles—about 109 times the diameter of Earth. This star is the most important one to us because it gives Earth heat and light. Yet it is dangerous to look directly at the Sun even if you are wearing sunglasses. Its rays are so strong that they can damage a person's eyesight or cause blindness.

The Moon: The Moon, Earth's only natural satellite, is our nearest neighbor in space (a *satellite* is any object that travels around another). This satellite, which is only about one-quarter the size of Earth, is made of rocks and dust. There are many mountains and craters on the Moon, but it has no air, wind, water, or life of any kind. The Moon is the brightest object in the night sky, yet it does not give off any light of its own. It reflects light from the Sun. The amount of light reflected differs, depending on the position of Earth, the Moon, and the Sun. These differences cause the Moon to appear to change shape. The varying shapes of the Moon are called *phases.* In 1969 the Moon became the first object in space to be visited by humans.

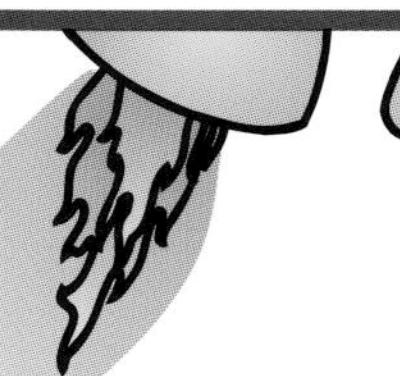

Introducing The Lesson:

Ask for three student volunteers. Explain that these students will demonstrate the *orbits,* or paths, of Earth and the Moon. Have the first youngster hold the Sun card in an open area of the classroom. Then have the second child hold the Earth card and walk once around the "Sun" in a large circle. Next ask the third volunteer to hold the Moon card and walk around "Earth" in a smaller circle. For an added challenge, have "Earth" and "Moon" orbit at the same time. Repeat this demonstration with different volunteers if desired. Discuss with youngsters the relative positions and paths of the Sun, the Moon, and Earth that were shown with this exercise. Tell students that they will learn more about the Sun and Moon with the following activity.

Steps:

1. Ask students to brainstorm information about the Sun and the Moon as you record their responses on the chart paper in the appropriate columns. Share the Background Information on page 59; then ask youngsters to help you add any new information to the brainstormed lists. Compare and contrast the two completed lists with students.
2. Give each student a copy of page 61. Tell youngsters that each of them will make a booklet about the Sun and the Moon.

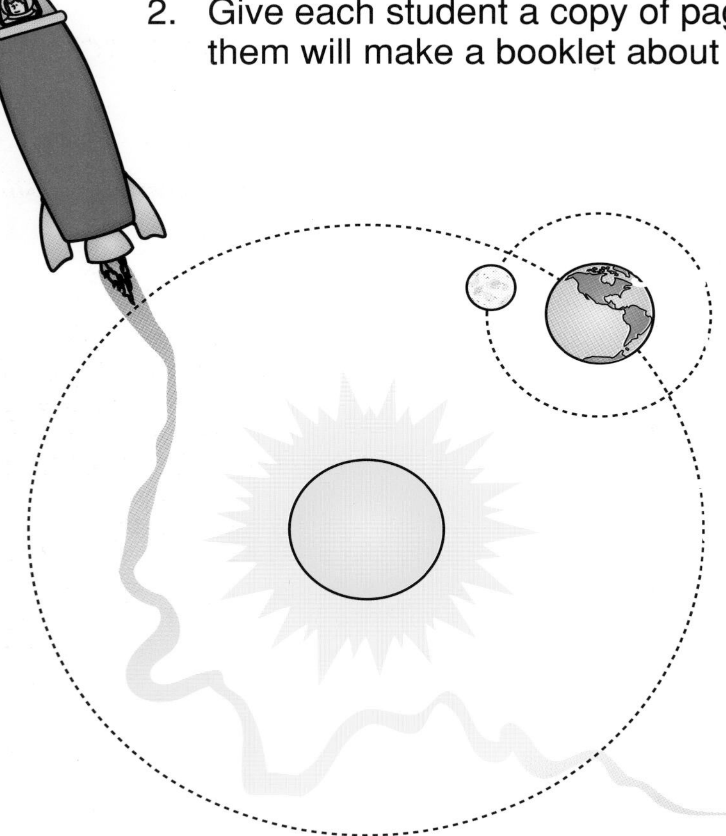

3. Read page 61 with students. Explain that they will need to complete each sentence with the most appropriate word from the Word Bank. Review the Word Bank words with youngsters.
4. Have each student complete the sentences on his sheet as directed, then personalize his booklet cover and pages.
5. Instruct each student to cut out, compile, and staple together his completed cover and pages.
6. After reading the resulting booklets, invite youngsters to take them home to share with their families.

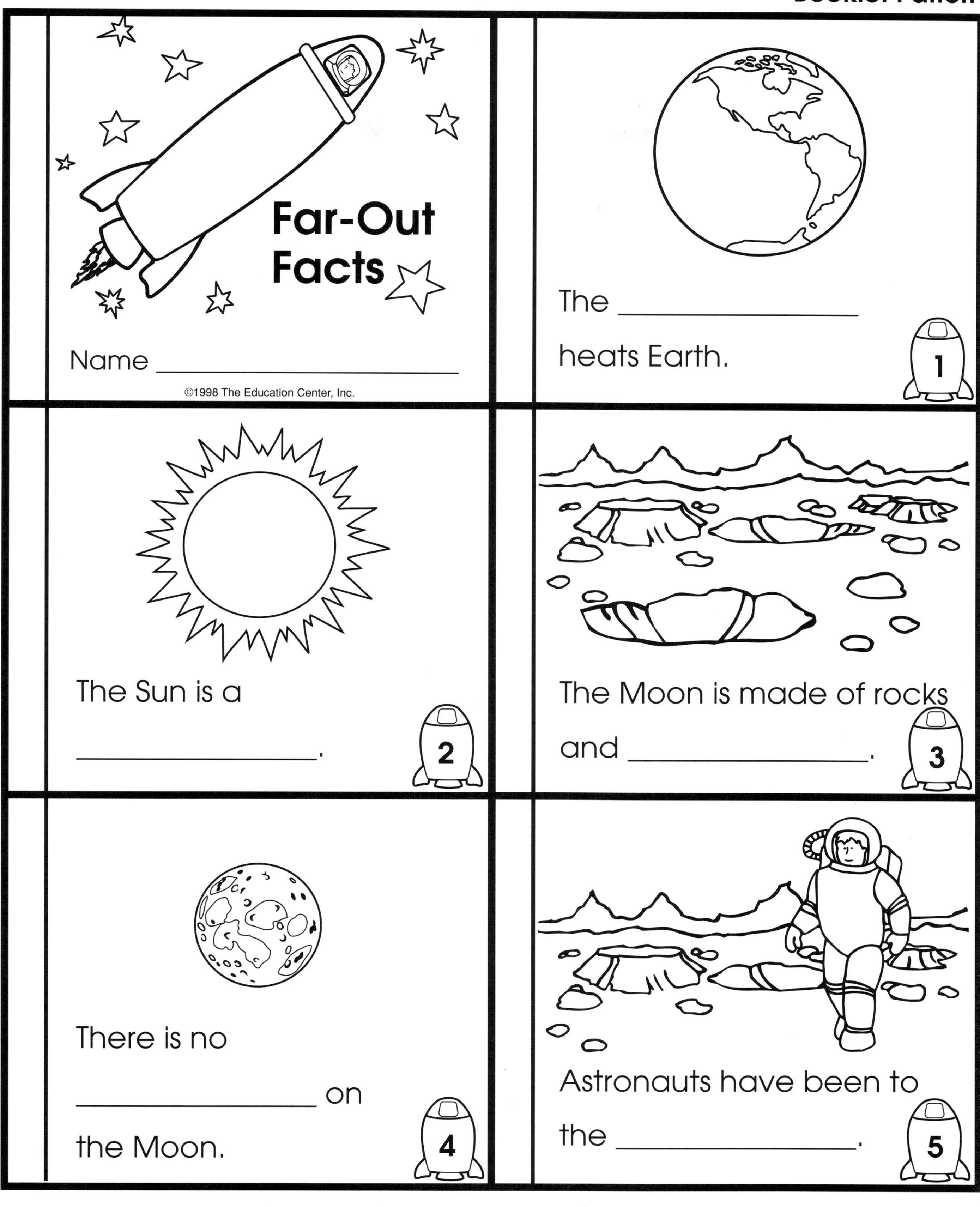

Word Bank

Moon star dust Sun air

How To Extend The Lesson:

- Imagination will take flight with this astronomical activity! Read aloud a book about traveling in space, such as *Floating In Space* by Franklyn M. Branley (HarperCollins Children's Books, 1998). Then invite each youngster to imagine that he is an astronaut traveling to the Moon. Have each child write a story about his adventures in an astronaut-shaped booklet. Encourage students to include facts about the Moon's gravity and the work that astronauts do in space, as well as other interesting information. Give youngsters an opportunity to read aloud their completed stories before showcasing this lunar literature in your classroom library.

- Rocket students into reading with these super space books!
  - — *Moongame* by Frank Asch (Simon & Schuster Children's Division, 1987)
  - — *The Magic School Bus Lost In The Solar System* by Joanna Cole (Scholastic Inc., 1994)
  - — *Why The Sun And The Moon Live In The Sky* by Elphinstone Dayrell (Houghton Mifflin Company, 1990)
  - — *What The Sun Sees, What The Moon Sees* by Nancy Tafuri (Greenwillow Books, 1997)

- Introduce students to some of the Moon's phases with this sequencing activity. Remind youngsters that the Moon appears to change shape because of the varying amount of light it reflects. Draw simple diagrams on your chalkboard to illustrate a crescent, first-quarter, gibbous, and full Moon. Also tell youngsters that a new Moon is not visible to us because the Moon is almost directly between the Sun and Earth during this phase. Then give each youngster four white-paper circles. Have him cut one to resemble each of the following phases: crescent, first-quarter, and gibbous. (The fourth circle will be a full Moon.) Next direct each youngster to sequence his four circles to show phases of the Moon on a strip of black paper. Also ask each child to leave space to represent a new Moon. If desired, have each youngster identify each of his Moon phases with small white labels. Follow up this activity by having each youngster keep a Moon diary. To keep a diary, he draws and dates an illustration of the Moon each day for a designated period of time.

A Rock-Solid Investigation

With this gem of a lesson, your students will gain a crystal-clear understanding of the properties of rocks and minerals!

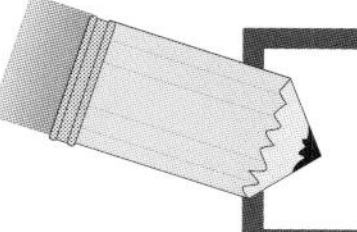

Skill: Observing and classifying rocks and minerals

Estimated Lesson Time: 45 minutes

Teacher Preparation:

1. Collect five or six rocks of various shapes, sizes, textures, and colors.
2. Duplicate page 65 for each student.

Materials:

1 rock per student collected during the "Rock Walk" (page 64)
1 penny per student
1 copy of page 65 per student

Background Information:

A rock is made of one or more minerals, such as iron, copper, silver, and chalk. Some of the distinguishing characteristics used to identify minerals are described below.

Luster: Luster refers to the way a mineral reflects light. Luster may be described as shiny, dull, metallic, earthy, greasy, or pearly.

Color: Most minerals can be found in several different colors because of impurities. A streak test gives information about a mineral's true color. (The color and streak of a mineral are not usually the same.) To do a streak test, rub a rock on a hard surface, such as the back of a ceramic tile or a concrete sidewalk. If the rock does not make a streak, it is harder than the surface.

Hardness: The hardness of a mineral is its resistance to being scratched. The *Mohs hardness scale* shows the relative hardness of ten common minerals. On this scale, number 1 is the softest mineral and number 10 is the hardest. A mineral can scratch any material with a lower hardness number. To test a rock for hardness, try to scratch it with a mineral or material of known hardness; then compare the results with the Mohs scale to identify it. For example, a penny has a hardness of 3 1/2 and can scratch calcite, talc, and gypsum. In contrast, a fingernail has a hardness of 2 1/2 and can scratch only very soft minerals such as talc and gypsum.

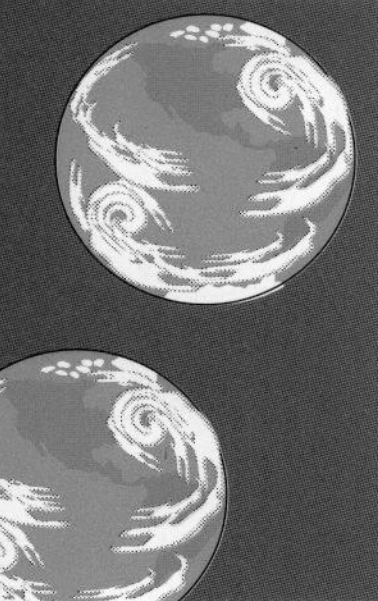

Introducing The Lesson:

Show students the rocks that you collected and have youngsters describe each rock's color, shape, texture, and other distinguishing features. Then sort the rocks into groups and have students determine how you categorized them. For example, you might categorize rocks according to color or sort rocks into groups of those that are shiny and those that are not. After students have correctly identified your sorting rule, continue in a similar manner with different groupings.

Steps:

1. Take students on a "Rock Walk" around your school. Instruct each youngster to look for rocks that have unique qualities and to choose one rock to bring back to the classroom.

2. Share the Background Information on page 63. Explain to students that they will observe some of these rock characteristics.

3. Divide students into groups of four or five. Provide each student with a copy of page 65 and a penny.

4. Have each youngster examine his rock and complete the first row of his chart. Then direct students to trade rocks with their group members in order to complete the next two rows with different rocks.

5. Instruct team members to place their rocks together so that they are visible to all members of the group. Have each student, in turn, tell his teammates the distinguishing features of one of the rocks that he observed; then challenge his teammates to identify the rock.

6. Discuss with youngsters the results of this identification activity. Were students able to readily match each description with the corresponding rock?

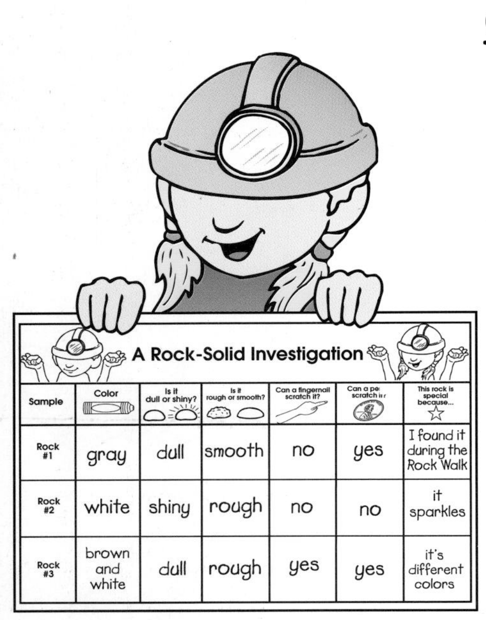

A Rock-Solid Investigation

Sample	Color	Is it dull or shiny?	Is it rough or smooth?	Can a fingernail scratch it?	Can a pe[illegible] scratch i[illegible]	This rock is special because...
Rock #1	gray	dull	smooth	no	yes	I found it during the Rock Walk
Rock #2	white	shiny	rough	no	no	it sparkles
Rock #3	brown and white	dull	rough	yes	yes	it's different colors

Name ____________________

A Rock-Solid Investigation

Sample	Color	Is it dull or shiny?	Is it rough or smooth?	Can a fingernail scratch it?	Can a penny scratch it?	This rock is special because... ☆
Rock #1						
Rock #2						
Rock #3						

How To Extend The Lesson:

- Tell students that an acid test helps determine the identity of a mineral. Have each youngster perform this test on a rock by placing a few drops of vinegar on it. Invite students to share their results. Explain that rocks containing carbonate will cause the vinegar to bubble and fizz. Have students use their findings from the acid test to sort their rocks into two groups—those with carbonate and those without.

- Remind students that minerals can be found in several different colors. Challenge each youngster to determine the true color of a rock by doing a streak test. To do this test, each child rubs a rock on an unglazed porcelain tile, a concrete sidewalk, or the back of a ceramic tile. After students have completed the streak test, have them group rocks that leave the same color streak and compare their appearances.

- Teach youngsters about rock formation by journeying to the center of the earth aboard The Magic School Bus®! Read aloud *The Magic School Bus Inside The Earth* by Joanna Cole (Scholastic Inc., 1989). This fanciful book explains that sedimentary rocks are formed from dust or sand settling in lakes and oceans; metamorphic rocks are formed by heat and pressure; and igneous rocks are formed when melted rock is pushed up through the earth's crust. At the conclusion of this story, show students a rock sample from each of these categories, such as sandstone (sedimentary), marble (metamorphic), and granite (igneous). Have youngsters share information they learned from the story as you record it on a large, bus-shaped piece of bulletin-board paper. Display this busload of facts on a classroom wall or bulletin board to serve as a handy reference throughout your study of rocks and minerals.

Science That Really Matters!

It's a matter of fact that students will enjoy studying solids, liquids, and gases with this thought-provoking activity.

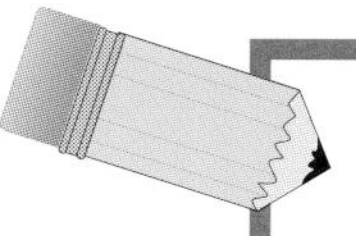

Skill: Classifying solids, liquids, and gases

Estimated Lesson Time: 30 minutes

Teacher Preparation:

1. Pour water into a glass until the glass is nearly full.
2. From discarded magazines, cut out approximately six pictures that show a variety of solids, liquids, and gases.
3. Draw three columns on a sheet of chart paper. Label one column "solids," another column "liquids," and the other column "gases."
4. Duplicate page 69 for each student.

Materials:

1 glass
water
several marbles (If marbles are unavailable, dried beans, such as kidney beans, are a suitable alternative.)
chart paper
several discarded magazines
one 9" x 12" sheet of construction paper per student
1 copy of page 69 per student
scissors
paper towels
glue
tape

Background Information:

All objects consist of matter and occupy space. Matter commonly exists in three different states—solid, liquid, and gas.

Solid: A solid has a distinct shape and resists change in shape.

Liquid: A liquid has no shape of its own and takes the shape of the container that holds it.

Gas: Gases are not usually visible. A gas has no definite shape and can expand indefinitely.

Introducing The Lesson:

Have students name several classroom objects. List the objects on the chalkboard. Tell students that these items have something in common—they are all matter. Explain that matter is anything that occupies space and has weight. Challenge students to think of things that are not matter. Feelings and thoughts are good examples.

Steps:

1. Show students the glass of water. (Make certain there is enough water in the glass so that adding the marbles to it will cause the water to overflow. Also place the paper towels within easy reach.) Tell students that you are going to add marbles to the glass. Have youngsters predict what will happen.

2. Drop the marbles into the glass a few at a time until the water overflows.

3. Engage students in a discussion about the results. Lead youngsters to the conclusion that both the marbles and water take up space and there isn't enough space in the glass for both the marbles and the water. Remind students that all matter occupies space; then share the additional Background Information on page 67.

4. Show students one of the magazine pictures, and have a student volunteer classify it as a solid, liquid, or gas. Have the youngster tape it onto the chart in the appropriate column. Continue in the same manner with the remaining pictures.

5. Distribute page 69 and a sheet of construction paper to each student. Help youngsters identify each of the pictured objects. Be sure to explain that gas isn't visible and that the illustrations of gases include lines that we don't normally see. Also tell students that some pictures have arrows to indicate the part of the picture that youngsters need to classify.

6. Direct each student to cut out the title and glue it to the top of his construction paper. Next have him cut out the labels and glue them below the title. Instruct each child to cut out his pictures and glue them in the appropriate columns.

Name ____________________ *Classifying solids, liquids, and gases*

Science That Really Matters!

Cut out the title and headings. Glue onto construction paper.
Cut out the pictures. Glue under the correct heading.

How To Extend The Lesson:

- Conduct a class experiment to determine which form of water takes up more space—liquid or solid. Completely fill with water a plastic container that has a lid. Ask the students to predict if the water will occupy more, less, or an equal amount of space when it freezes. Place the lid on the container; then place it in the freezer. Retrieve the container when the water is frozen, and display the container for all to see. Discuss the results with students. (The container will bulge and the lid may pop off the container because ice occupies more space than water.)

- Looking for hands-on activities to help your youngsters explore the three states of matter? Then be sure to share *Solids, Liquids And Gases* by The Ontario Science Centre (Kids Can Press Ltd., 1998). Each of the 13 activities contains a materials list, instructions, and an explanation. There is also a special page for teachers that provides additional activities and information.

- A study of the water cycle is a great way to teach the states of matter. Read aloud *The Water's Journey* by Eleonore Schmid (North-South Books Inc., 1994). Discuss how the snow in the book transformed throughout the story. First it melted, changing from a solid to a liquid. The water flowed into a stream and then into a lake. Water evaporated from the lake and became a gas. When the water vapor cooled, it became droplets of water. The book concludes by stating that the droplets will fall back down to earth again in the form of rain or snow, and the cycle will continue. After the discussion, enlist students' help to create a class diagram of the water cycle similar to the one shown.

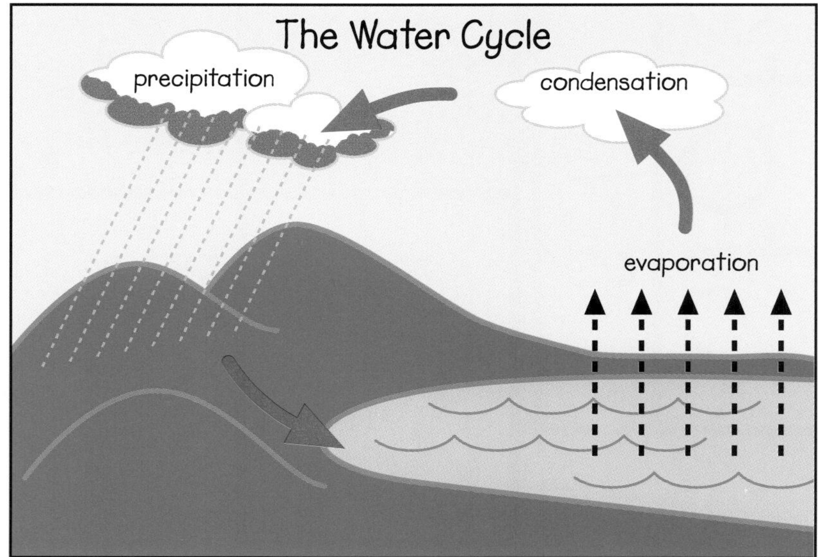

Sink Or Float?

Set your youngsters afloat with this hands-on science activity.

Skill: Determining whether objects sink or float

Estimated Lesson Time: 30 minutes

Teacher Preparation:

1. Fill a clear container with water.
2. Gather the materials listed below.
3. Duplicate page 73 for each student.
4. Duplicate one sink and one float card (on page 74) for each student.

Materials:

clear container (with a wide lid) filled with water
one sink and one float card per student
1 copy of page 73 per student
rubber band
crayon
paper clip
scissors
penny
pencil
ruler
chalk
key

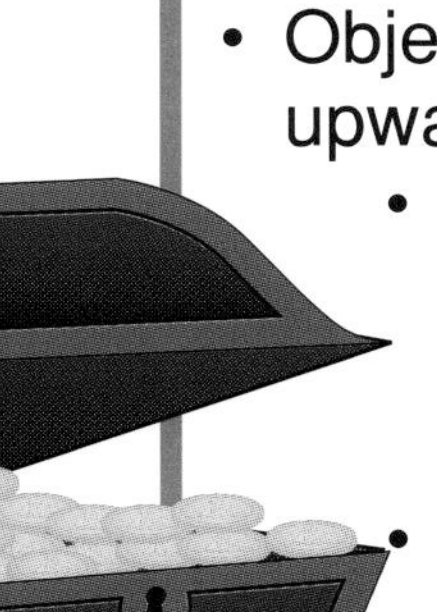

Background Information:

- When an object is placed in water, it displaces (pushes) some of the water away.
- Objects that displace more water than their own weight float.
- Objects that do not have enough upward push from the water sink.
    - Salt water is heavier than fresh water. There is more upward push to float heavier objects in salt water.
    - A raw egg will float in a cup of salt water and sink in a cup of fresh water.

Introducing The Lesson:

Ask your youngsters to imagine a mermaid is swimming at the bottom of the ocean and finds a treasure chest. She opens the treasure chest and finds it full of coins. She takes one of the coins out of the chest and drops it. Ask students to think about whether the coin will sink or float.

Steps:

1. Provide each child with one sink card and one float card. To test the coin prediction, ask each child to indicate whether she thinks the coin will sink or float by holding up the corresponding sink or float card. Ask student volunteers to explain their predictions. Do more children think the penny will float, or do more think it will sink?

2. Have a child drop the penny into the water. Ask a student volunteer to shore the result of the experiment.

3. If desired share the Background Information on page 71.

4. Distribute a copy of page 73 to each student. Instruct students to complete only the prediction section of the reproducible. (Based on their predictions, students color either the sink or the float box on their papers.)

5. As a whole-group activity, ask student volunteers to help you test the objects listed on the reproducible to determine whether each one sinks or floats. Have students record the answers in the column labeled "Results" on the reproducible.

6. Challenge students to complete the Bonus Box activity.

Name ______________________________

Sink Or Float?

Predict and color.
Test and write results.

	Object	Prediction		Results
		Sink	Float	
1.	pencil			
2.	rubber band			
3.	crayon			
4.	paper clip			
5.	ruler			
6.	chalk			
7.	scissors			
8.	key			

Bonus Box: On the back of this sheet, write three other objects that float and three other objects that sink.

How To Extend The Lesson:

- Show a piece of cotton to your students. Have them predict whether the cotton will sink or float when you place it in water. Then drop the cotton into a container of water. The cotton will float for a few seconds; then it will sink to the bottom. Explain to students that the weight of the cotton increases as it absorbs water, making it harder to stay afloat.

- Set up a sink-or-float center in your classroom. Fill a large container with water. Place several objects—half of which sink in water and half of which float in water—at the center. Have small groups of students take turns visiting the center to test each object's buoyancy.

- Have students make clay boats. Provide each student with a ball of oil-based clay. Instruct each student to mold her clay into the shape of a boat. Then have students test their boats to determine if they float.

- Perform the following ice-cube experiment in your classroom. Place a few ice cubes in a glass. Ask a student to try to cover the ice cubes by pouring water on them. Students will be amazed to see that the cubes will not stay under the water. The cubes keep coming up to the top of the glass. Explain to students that ice cubes float on water because they are lighter than water.

Sink Or Float Cards

Use with Step 1 on page 72.

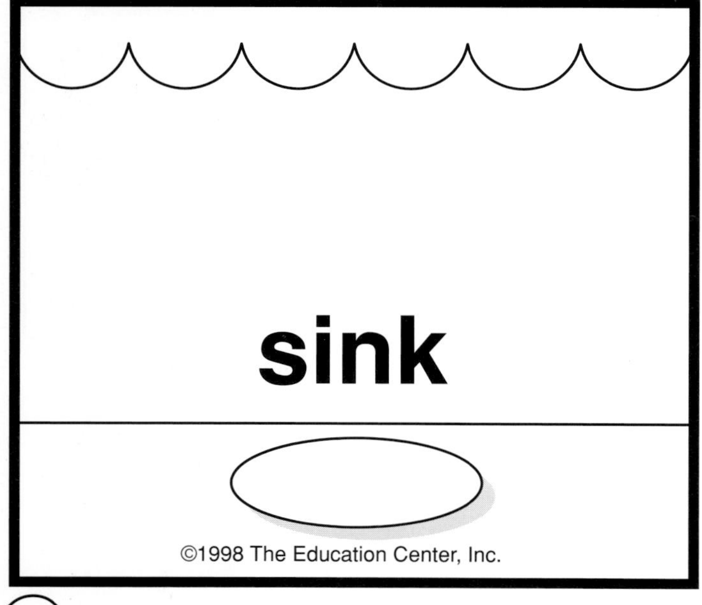

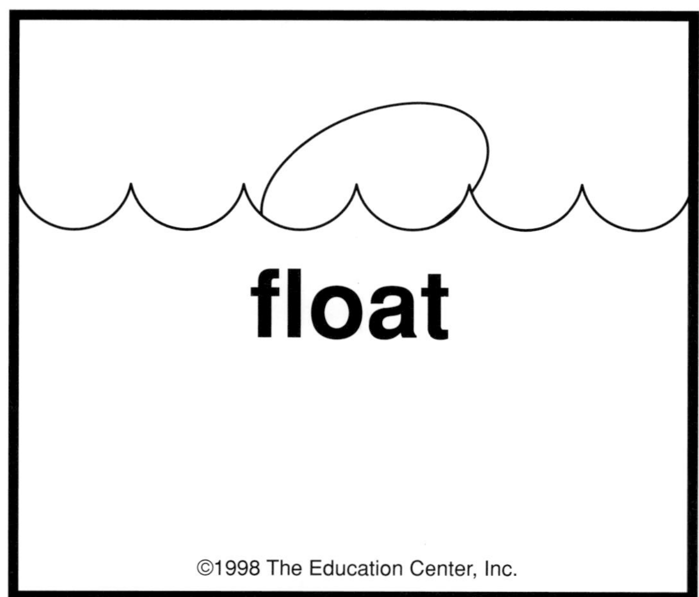

Magnet Mania

Attract your students with these magnificent magnet experiments!

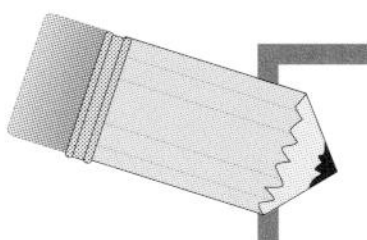

Skill: Identifying magnetic objects

Estimated Lesson Time: 30 minutes

Teacher Preparation:

1. Duplicate page 77 for each student.
2. Tie a string to a paper clip for each student pair.
3. Divide the listed materials (except the paper clip with string attached) into a separate container for each student pair.
4. Make two columns on your chalkboard. Label one column "Magnetic" and the other "Nonmagnetic."

Materials:

1 copy of page 77 per student
1 magnet per student pair
1 paper clip with string attached per student pair
1 of each of the following items per student pair: penny, nickel, dime, iron nail, metal spoon, crayon, key, metal scissors, screw, and small piece of aluminum foil
1 small container per student pair

Background Information:

- The ancient Greeks and Romans noticed that a particular kind of black stone had a magnetic force. One legend about this stone tells about a shepherd from Magnesia. He discovered that his metal-tipped staff was attracted to this type of stone. He named this stone "magnet" after his homeland. Today we call this stone *iron ore.*
- At the end of the 16th century, William Gilbert studied magnets. He suggested that Earth itself is a magnet. Today's scientists agree and believe that Earth's inner core is made of iron and nickel.
- Magnets attract iron and steel objects. We use magnets for many things in our daily lives. Magnets are used in radios, videocassette recorders, telephones, and compasses. The first compasses were probably made of lodestone, which means "leading stone." The needle of a compass always points north because it is pulled by Earth's magnetism.

Introducing The Lesson:

Tell students that you have a challenge for them. To prepare for the task, divide students into pairs. Give each student pair a magnet and a paper clip that has a string attached. Direct each student pair to rest its paper clip on a desktop. Then challenge each pair of youngsters to move the paper clip across the desktop without touching the string or paper clip. Engage the children in a discussion about the results. How did they accomplish the task? What enabled them to be successful? Collect the materials used.

Steps:

1. Introduce the term *magnetic* and explain that a magnet pulls iron and steel objects toward it. Then share the additional Background Information provided on page 75.

2. Have students continue to work in pairs and give each student pair a container of materials. Direct youngsters to examine the objects in their containers. Challenge students to determine similarities and differences among the items. Ask youngsters to share their observations with the class.

3. Tell students that they will complete an experiment to examine one particular characteristic of the items—magnetism.

4. Give each child a copy of page 77. Have him predict whether or not each of the listed objects is magnetic. Instruct each youngster to record his predictions by making *X*s in the appropriate boxes on his sheet.

5. Provide a magnet for each student pair. Direct students to test their predictions and record their results on their sheets.

6. After all your students have completed the experiment, enlist their help in compiling lists of magnetic and nonmagnetic items on the chalkboard. Assist students in analyzing the list and making generalizations about magnetic and nonmagnetic objects.

Magnetic	Nonmagnetic
metal spoon	crayon
metal scissors	penny

Name ______________________________ *Identifying magnetic objects*

Magnet Mania

Predict whether or not each object is magnetic.
Draw an *X* in each of the appropriate boxes.
Test.
Record your results.

	Object	Prediction		Results ☺ or ☹
		Magnetic	Nonmagnetic	
1.	spoon			
2.	penny			
3.	nickel			
4.	dime			
5.	nail			
6.	crayon			
7.	key			
8.	screw			
9.	scissors			
10.	foil			

How To Extend The Lesson

- Give each student a magnet for this take-home assignment. Instruct him to use the magnet at home to find as many magnetic items as possible. Have each child share his findings with the class the next day. Record youngsters' responses on chart paper and discuss the results.

- Have students explore the strength of different magnets with this activity. For each group of students, provide a few different types of magnets, such as bar, horseshoe, and wand magnets. Instruct students to predict how many paper clips each of the magnets will hold. Then ask students to test their predictions.

- Share these marvelous magnet books with your youngsters. All three books contain magnet experiments that are sure to delight your students!
  —*Playing With Magnets: With Easy-To-Make Scientific Projects* by Gary Gibson (The Millbrook Press, Inc.; 1995)
  —*Science Magic With Magnets* by Chris Oxlade (Barron's Educational Series, Inc.; 1994)
  —*What Makes A Magnet?* by Franklyn M. Branley (HarperCollins Children's Books, 1996)

- Tell students that some animals—such as pigeons, honeybees, salmon, tuna, dolphins, and turtles—have magnetite in their bodies. Scientists believe that these creatures detect and use Earth's magnetic field to help find their way. Have students explore this information with the following maze activity. For each child, create and duplicate the maze and turtle pattern shown. Instruct each youngster to color and cut out the turtle, then tape a paper clip underneath his turtle. Next have him adhere a strip of magnetic tape to a wooden craft stick. To begin, the student places the turtle on his paper at the beginning of the maze. Then he places the craft-stick magnet under his paper and uses it to guide the turtle through the maze. For added fun, have students create different maze backgrounds and characters.

Simple-Machine Match

Students will put their classification skills into high gear with this machine matching game!

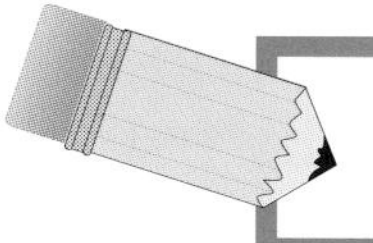

Skill: Classifying simple machines (wheel and axle, lever, and inclined plane)

Estimated Lesson Time: 45 minutes

Teacher Preparation:

1. Duplicate page 81 for each student.
2. Make a set of 15 flash cards. Label five of the cards "inclined plane," five "lever," and five "wheel and axle."
3. Gather items to demonstrate a lever, a wheel and axle, and an inclined plane. (See the introduction on page 80.)

Materials:

1 copy of page 81 per student
15 game markers per student
1 set of simple-machine flash cards
container for flash cards
glue
scissors
materials to demonstrate a lever, a wheel and axle, and an inclined plane

Background Information:

There are six types of simple machines—inclined plane, lever, pulley, wheel and axle, screw, and wedge. All machines are based on one or more of these simple machines.

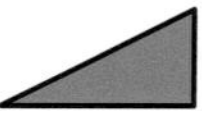

- The **inclined plane** helps raise an object a greater height with less effort than it would require unaided. One type of inclined plane is a ramp.

- The **lever** also allows us to lift a load with less effort. It is positioned on a pivotal point called a fulcrum. Seesaws and crowbars are levers.

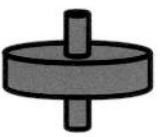

- The **wheel and axle** work together to disperse force. A wheel can move a great distance with little effort. Examples of a wheel and axle are a bicycle, a screwdriver, a steering wheel, and a wrench and bolt.

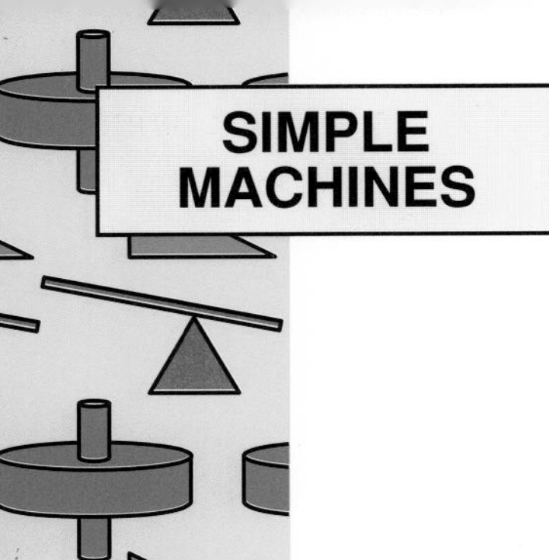

Introducing The Lesson:

Explain to students that machines make work easier. Then tell youngsters that they will play a game that features three types of simple machines—wheel and axle, inclined plane, and lever. These machines are found in many common objects. Demonstrate how each of the featured simple machines works by using common objects such as a pencil sharpener (wheel and axle), a ramp and toy car (inclined plane), and a balance scale (lever).

Steps:

1. Share the Background Information on page 79.

2. Distribute a copy of page 81 to each student. Review with students the pictures at the bottom of their papers. Direct students to cut out the picture cards. Have each child glue the cards onto his gameboard in random order.

3. Distribute the game markers and place the premade simple-machine flash cards in the container. Announce the type of game to be played, such as three in a row, four corners, or five in a row.

4. To play Simple-Machine Match, draw a flash card and announce the type of machine listed on the card. Have each student find a corresponding picture on his gameboard, and direct him to cover the space with a game marker.

5. The first student to cover the gameboard spaces needed to win calls "Simple-Machine Match!" Then he verifies his win by identifying the machines that he covered. The winner becomes the caller.

6. To begin a new game, ask students to clear their gameboards. Place the flash cards back in the container, and invite the winner of the previous game to be the caller.

Name ______________________________

Simple-Machine Match

Cut.
Glue.
Follow your teacher's directions.

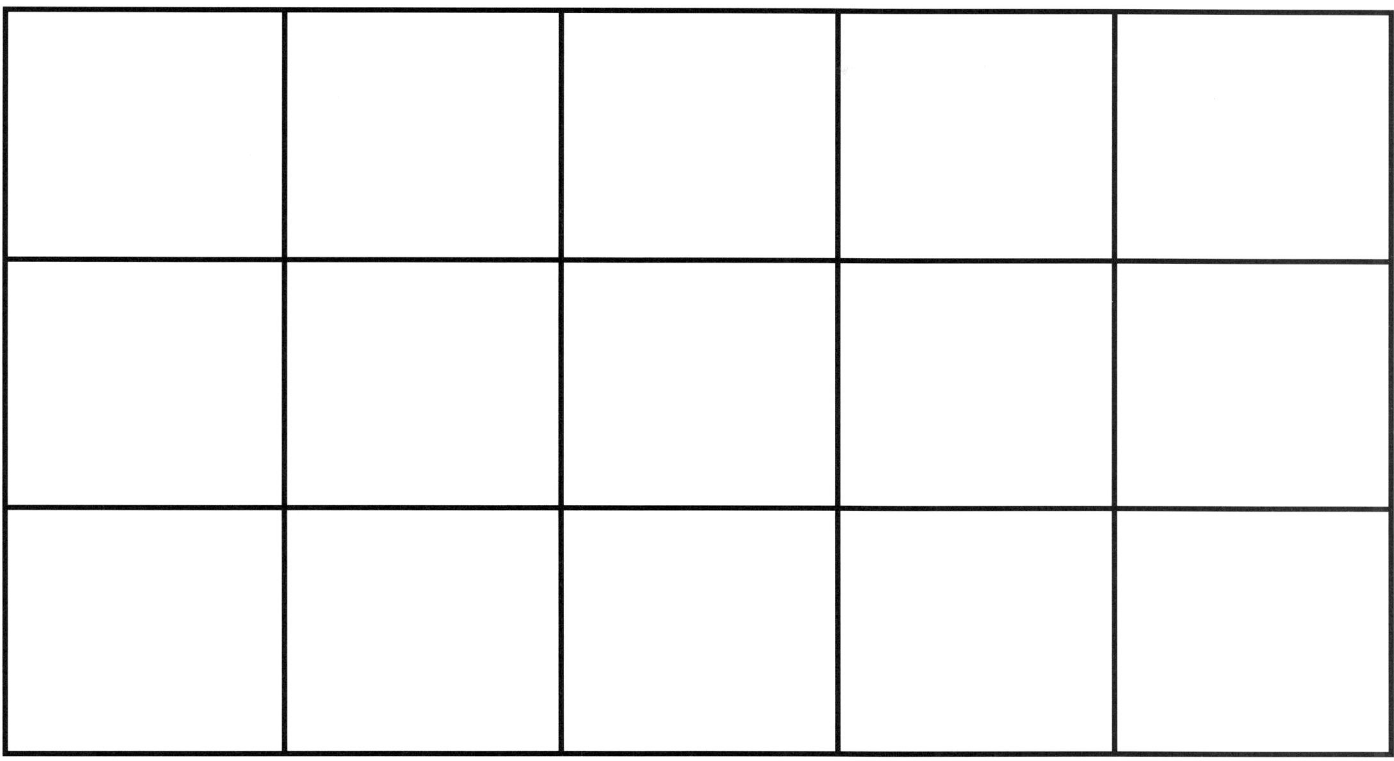

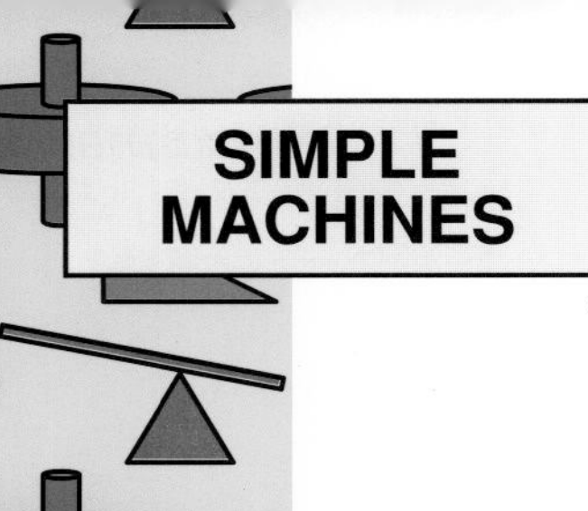

How To Extend The Lesson:

- Make a ramp at a center by resting a sheet of heavy cardboard on a block. Fill a container with several small objects that roll easily and several that do not. Marbles, pencils, coins, pattern blocks, sponges, and Unifix® cubes are good choices. Direct students who visit the center to determine which objects roll most easily. Have students study the speed of the rolling objects too.

- Give students an opportunity to experiment with one type of lever—a balance scale. At a center, place a balance scale, Unifix® cubes, and a box containing several small objects that vary in weight and density, such as a rock, a piece of cork, a box of crayons, and a glue bottle. A student visits the center and chooses an object from the box. Next he estimates how many Unifix® cubes are needed to equal the weight of the object. Then he experiments with the balance scale to determine the actual number of cubes required.

- Try this activity to demonstrate how common the wheel and axle is in our world. Have students work together in small groups to find and cut out several magazine pictures of a wheel and axle. Then have each group share its findings.

- Introduce students to the remaining types of simple machines—the pulley, screw, and wedge. Provide examples of each type of machine. Fishing reels and flagpoles are pulleys; corkscrews and lightbulb bases are screws; and knives, forks, and needles are wedges. Tell students that *compound machines* are made of two or more simple machines. Scissors, can openers, and hand drills are compound machines. Challenge students to identify the simple machines that each of these items contains.

- Award each student a construction-paper copy of the badge shown.

LEVER
I'M SIMPLY A MACHINE EXPERT
INCLINED PLANE
WHEEL AND AXLE

The Fabulous Five!

Entice your students' five senses with this "sense-sational" science lesson!

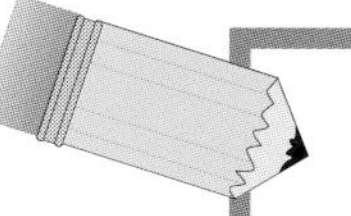

Skill: Identifying the five senses

Estimated Lesson Time: 45 minutes

Teacher Preparation:

1. On a sheet of bulletin-board paper, draw and label a web similar to the one shown.
2. Duplicate page 85 for each student.

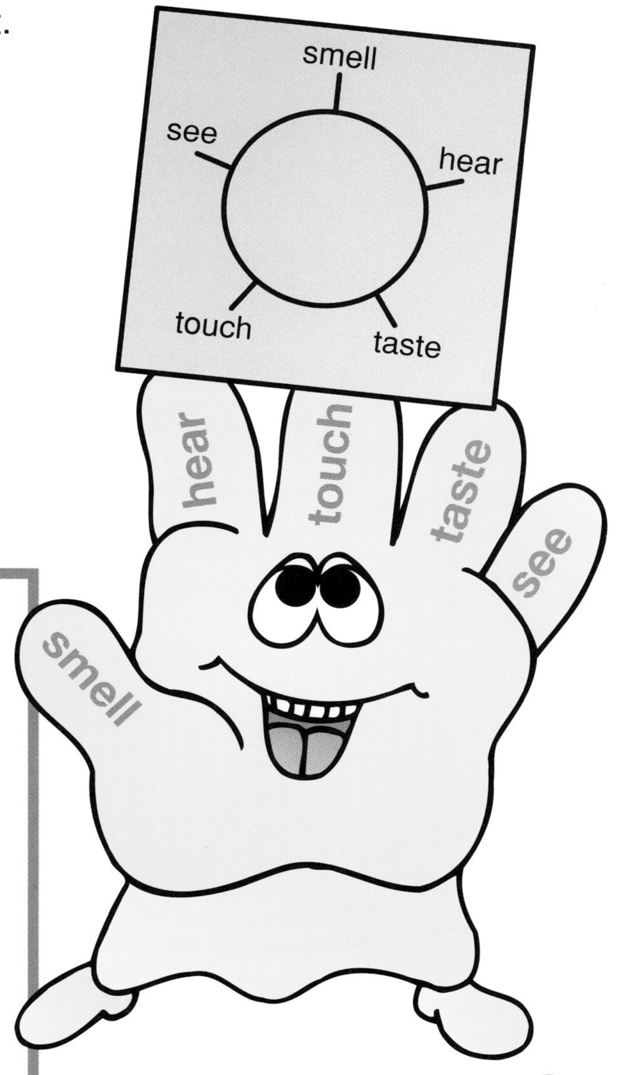

Materials:

1 sheet of bulletin-board paper
1 copy of page 85 per student
3 sheets of white paper per student
2 sheets of light-colored construction paper per student
glue
scissors
crayons
stapler

Background Information:

- The five senses—*hearing, sight, smell, taste,* and *touch*—are external senses. These senses tell us about things that occur far from the body and things that come in contact with it.
  - —The senses of hearing and sight tell us about things that happen far from the body.
  - —The senses of taste, touch, and smell tell us about things that come in contact with the body.

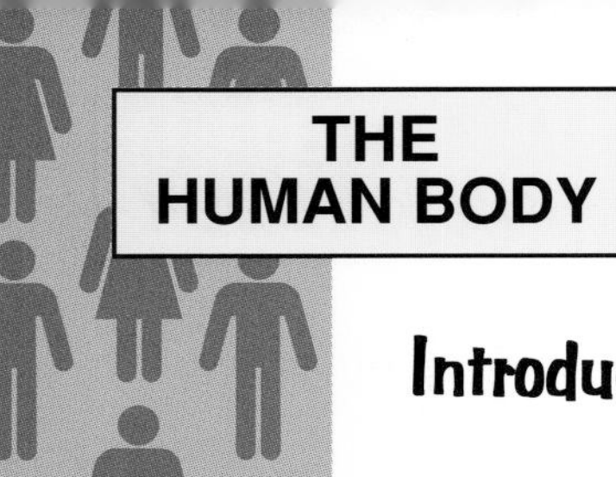

Introducing The Lesson:

Ask each child to close his eyes and think of a place that he enjoys visiting. Then ask him to imagine things that he could see, hear, touch, smell, and taste at this place. Be sure to do this activity yourself, also. After approximately a minute, ask students to open their eyes. Then tell them to remember this experience, because they will use the information to make a five-senses booklet.

Steps:

1. Display the web in a prominent location. Write the place you imagined visiting in the center of the web.

2. On the web, write a student-generated list of things that can be seen, touched, heard, smelled, and tasted at this place.

3. Share the Background Information on page 83 with students.

4. Distribute a copy of page 85, three sheets of duplicating paper, and two sheets of construction paper to each student. Instruct each student to use his memory of the place he imagined (in the introduction to the lesson) to fill in the blanks on the reproducible.

5. To make a five-senses booklet, a student cuts out the strips and glues each one (in numerical order) to the front or back of a sheet of duplicating paper. Next he compiles the pages in numerical order, staples them between the two construction-paper covers, and illustrates the pages to match the sentences. Finally he adds a title and decorations to the front cover of his booklet.

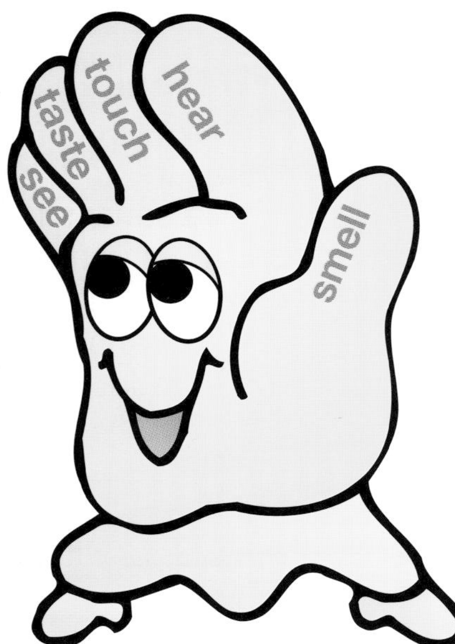

1. My favorite place is ____________________ because ____________________.

2. At ____________ I can ____________________.

3. At ____________ I can ____________________.

4. At ____________ I can ____________________.

5. At ____________ I can ____________________.

6. At ____________ I can ____________________.

How To Extend The Lesson:

- This activity is fast, easy, and tastes as good as it smells! When the children are out of the classroom, hide three or four open bags of freshly popped popcorn in different locations. When the students return, have them use their sense of smell to find the popcorn. Have students bring the bags to you as soon as they find them. When all of the bags have been found, provide each child with a handful of the tasty treat!

- Take your students on a listening walk through the school. Ask students to walk quietly with you through the building and listen for all kinds of sounds. Upon returning to the classroom, have students name the sounds that they heard on the walk. You will be amazed at the variety of sounds that the students identified and remembered!

- Send your youngsters on a touching safari! Divide students into small groups and select a recorder for each group. Instruct each group to find smooth, bumpy, hard, or soft objects in the classroom. Have the recorder from each group write down his group's findings. When the safari is over, invite the groups to share the items they found.

- This tasty activity will excite your students and their taste buds! In advance, design a reproducible (similar to the one shown) that states "Correct Guesses" in one column and "Incorrect Guesses" in another column. Place groups of two or three students around a plate of original flavor Skittles® candy. To begin, one student in each group closes his eyes, chooses a piece of candy, and places it in his mouth. After chewing slowly for a few seconds, the student guesses the flavor. The others in the group should tell him if the guess is correct. The student then makes a tally in the appropriate column of his tally sheet. Students repeat the activity until each member has had at least five turns.

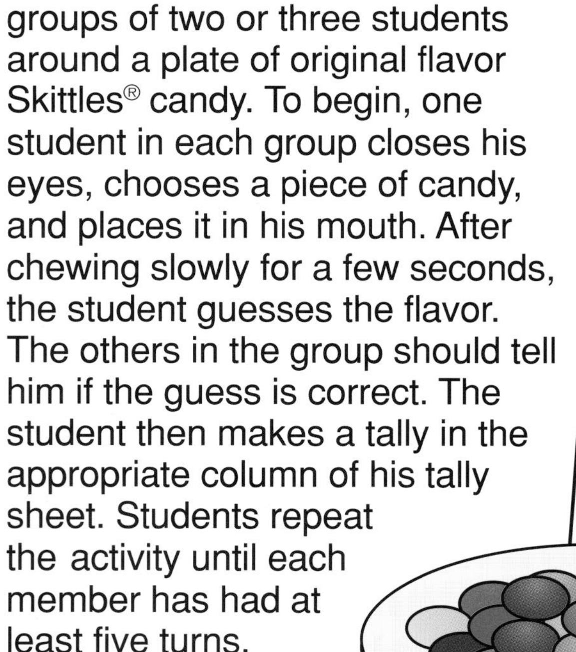

Nutty Over Nutrition!

Students will go nutty over nutrition with this lesson on making healthful food choices!

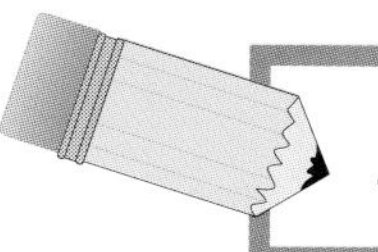

Skill: Making healthful food choices

Estimated Lesson Time: 45 minutes

Teacher Preparation:

1. Duplicate a copy of page 89 for each student.
2. Make an overhead transparency of page 89.
3. Divide a sheet of chart paper into three columns. Label the first column "Actions," the middle column "Healthful Snacks," and the last column "Unhealthful Snacks." Post the chart in a prominent location.

Materials:

1 copy of page 89 for each student
labeled chart
1 overhead transparency of page 89
overhead-projector marker
overhead projector
two 9" x 12" sheets of construction paper
crayons
markers
scissors
paper lunch bag
stapler

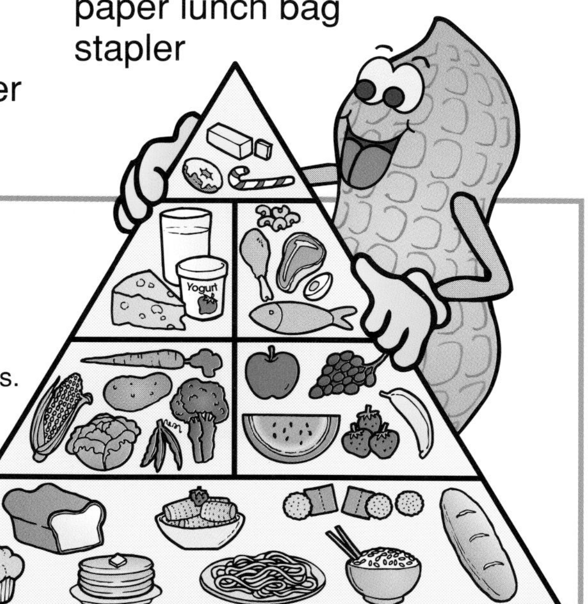

Background Information:

- Food serves many different functions. It provides:
  —energy for our actions,
  —substances for our bodies to build and repair tissues,
  —and substances for our bodies to regulate organs and systems.
- Our bodies need a variety of different foods to help them grow.
- Food choices and servings should be based on the Food Guide Pyramid (from the U.S. Dept. of Agriculture and the U.S. Dept. of Health and Human Services).

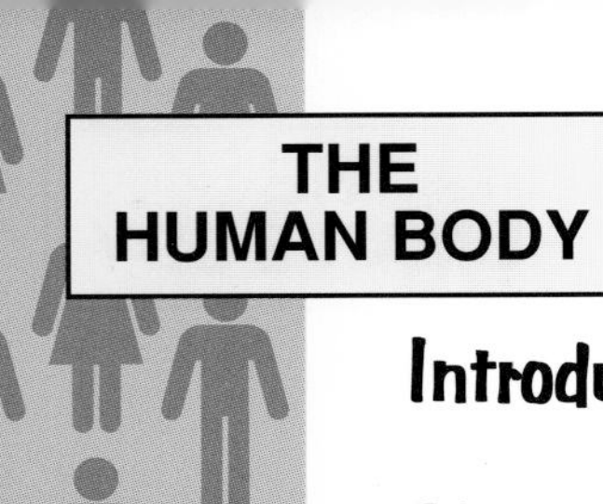

Introducing The Lesson:

Show your students a lunch bag and ask them to brainstorm what healthful snacks the lunch bag could contain. Record their responses under the column labeled "Healthful Snacks" on the chart. Next write a student-generated list of junk food under the column labeled "Unhealthful Snacks." In the column labeled "Actions," enlist students' help in listing several different ways food might be eaten (past-tense verbs). Consider words such as *devoured, ingested, gulped, chewed on, swallowed, feasted on,* and *bit into.* Then explain to students that they will be creating a "Nutty Over Nutrition" class flip book. Each student will be responsible for writing and illustrating a page.

Steps:

1. Discuss with students the Background Information and the Food Guide Pyramid on page 87. Ask student volunteers to explain the importance of choosing healthful snacks. Then review the students' healthful and unhealthful food choices on the chart paper. Enlist students' help in verifying that each food in the chart is in the appropriate column.

2. Place the transparency of page 89 onto the overhead. Show students how to use the chart to complete the blanks on the transparency. (See the example.)

3. Distribute a copy of page 89 to each student. Instruct each student to write her name, an action word(s), a healthful snack, and an unhealthful snack on the appropriate lines. Encourage students to choose words from the chart.

4. On the body outline, have each student illustrate herself holding her snack. (Ask girls not to draw themselves in skirts or dresses for the purpose of this activity.)

5. Collect and stack the pages. Cut along the dotted lines to create three strips on each paper. To make a class flip book, staple the pages between two construction-paper covers. Place the book in the classroom library. Encourage students to randomly flip the strips and read the resulting sentence from top to bottom.

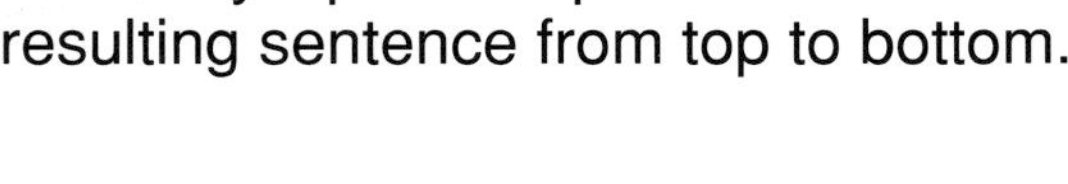

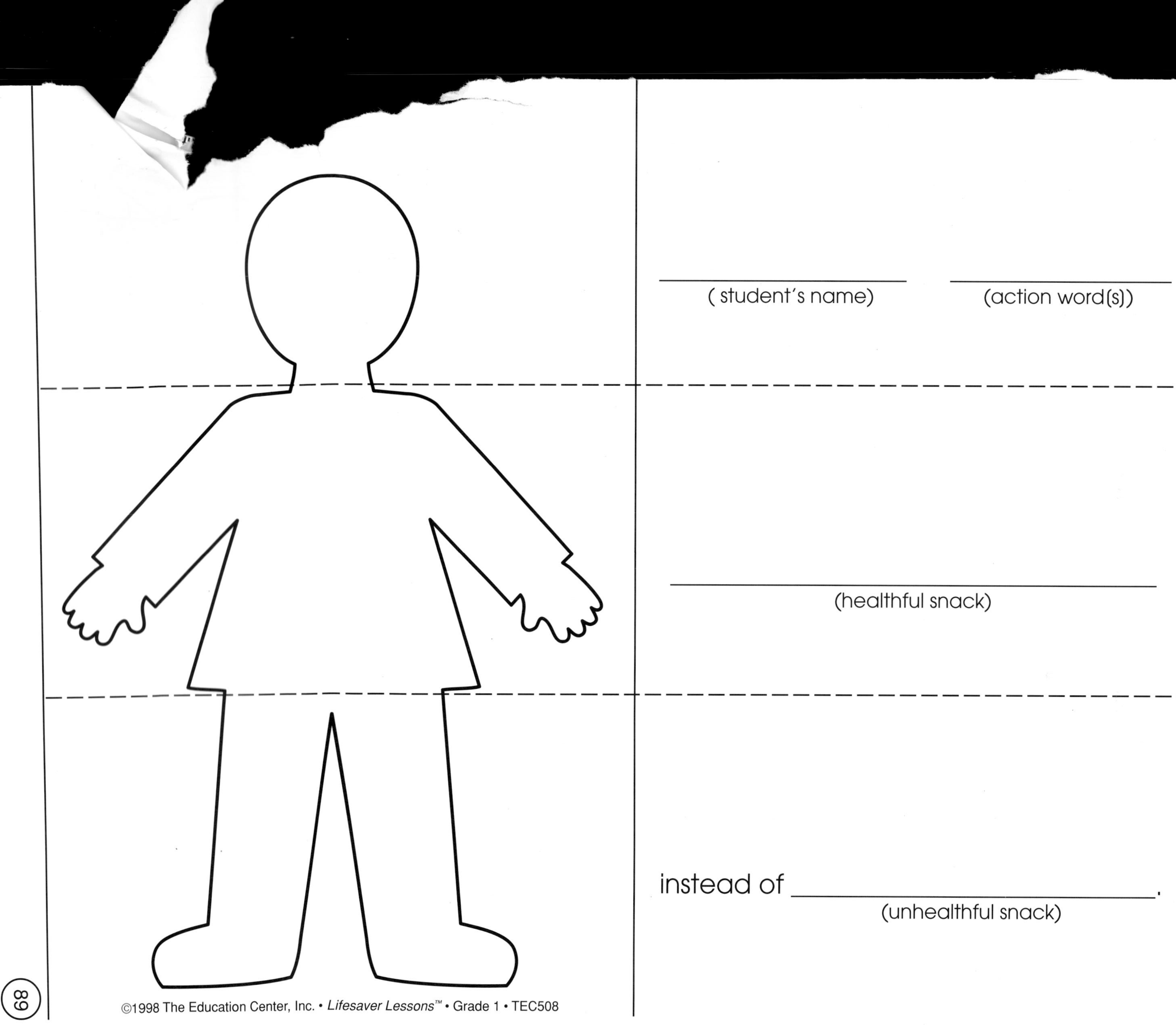

______________ ______________
(student's name) (action word(s))

____
(healthful snack)

instead of ______________________________.
(unhealthful snack)

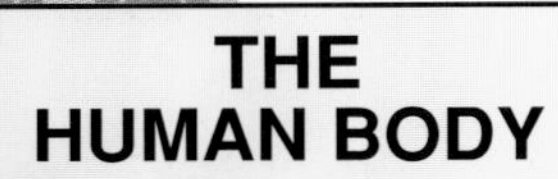

How To Extend The Lesson:

- Invite students to write snack riddles! Direct each student to pack a healthful snack from home and bring it to school the following day. Have each student write three clues about her top-secret snack on a large index card. (Be sure to tell the student to include the snack's food group as one of the clues.) Ask each student to share her clues, and encourage others to predict the contents of her snack bag. Provide time for youngsters to enjoy their snacks when all the riddles are solved!

- Remind students that peanuts are packed with nutrition. Explain that not only do they make an excellent snack, but when part of a balanced meal, they can take the place of one meat serving. Then invite each student to make the following "peanutty" snack.

  Nutty "Nannas": Place banana slices on forks, dip in yogurt or spread with peanut butter, and then roll in crushed peanuts.

- Reinforce students' understanding of the Food Guide Pyramid with this activity. To begin, divide a large triangle into six sections to create a Food Guide Pyramid. Label each section with its corresponding food group; then cut the triangle into six sections. Place students into six groups and give each group a section of the Food Guide Pyramid. Each group cuts food pictures from discarded magazines that correspond with its food group. Then the group glues the pictures to its Food Guide Pyramid section. Assemble the completed sections, and post the resulting pyramid on a wall or bulletin board. If desired invite students to bring in nutrition labels from healthful food products to display around the pyramid.

- Share the story *The Edible Pyramid: Good Eating Every Day* by Loreen Leedy (Holiday House, Inc.; 1996). Then challenge students to make picture-menus for breakfast, lunch, or dinner. To make a menu, a youngster draws and labels pictures of desired foods on provided paper. Remind students that at least four food groups need to be represented on their menus. For added fun, select a menu for a class snack party!

Tip-Top Teeth!

Brush up students' dental-health habits with this "tooth-rific" lesson!

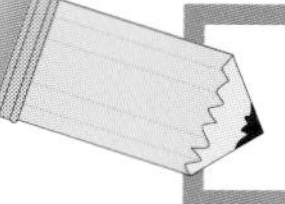

Skill: Recognizing healthful dental-health habits

Estimated Lesson Time: 30 minutes

Teacher Preparation:

1. On bulletin-board paper, draw a large smiley face similar to the one on page 92. (Do not include the teeth in the drawing.) Post the paper in a prominent location.
2. Cut out eight white rectangles (teeth) proportionately sized to the smiley face.
3. Label each rectangle (as shown on page 92) with one of the following statements.
   —Sugar is not good for your teeth.
   —Dental floss cleans between your teeth.
   —You should visit the dentist at least once a year.
   —Calcium helps to make teeth strong and healthy.
   —You should try to brush your teeth after every meal.
   —A *cavity* is an area of decay in a tooth.
   —Replace a toothbrush when the bristles are worn.
   —Replace sugary snacks with foods such as fruits, vegetables, and cheeses.
4. Duplicate page 93 for each student.

Materials:

bulletin-board paper (labeled with a smiley face)
1 copy of page 93 per student
tape
eight labeled tooth cutouts
access to as many mirrors as possible
(preferably handheld mirrors)

Background Information:

- There are four types of permanent teeth. Each type of tooth performs a different job.
  — The *incisors,* the chief biting teeth, are located at the front of the jaw.
  — *Canines,* or *cuspids,* are used with the incisors to bite into food. They are also used to tear off pieces of food. Canines are located at the sides of the jaw.
  — *Premolars,* sometimes called *bicuspids,* crush and grind food.
  — *Molars,* like premolars, grind food. They are shaped like premolars but are larger. Molars are located at the back of the jaw.

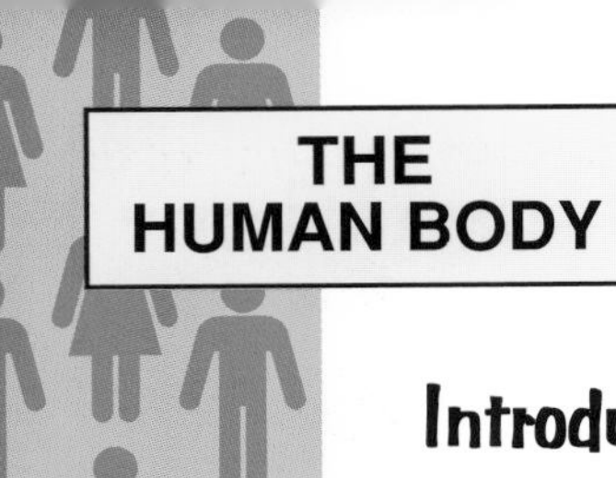

Introducing The Lesson:

Point to the smiley face on the bulletin-board paper. Tell students that the character is Mr. Smiley Face and that he needs their help. He needs them to give him some teeth. Explain to students that for each dental-health fact they review, they can give Mr. Smiley Face a tooth.

Steps:

1. For each labeled tooth cutout, ask a student volunteer to read (with your help) the dental-health statement. After reading each statement, have the student tape the tooth inside Mr. Smiley Face's mouth.

2. Review the Background Information on page 91 with students. Remind students that their permanent teeth may or may not have started to appear. Explain that between the ages of 6 and 12, a child has some permanent and some baby teeth in the mouth.

3. Divide students into as many groups as you have mirrors. Have the students in each group take turns looking at their teeth in the mirror. Encourage students to observe the different types of teeth they have and the number of teeth (if any) that are missing. After each student has had a chance to look at her teeth, collect the mirrors and remind students of the importance of toothbrushing, flossing, and eating a healthful diet.

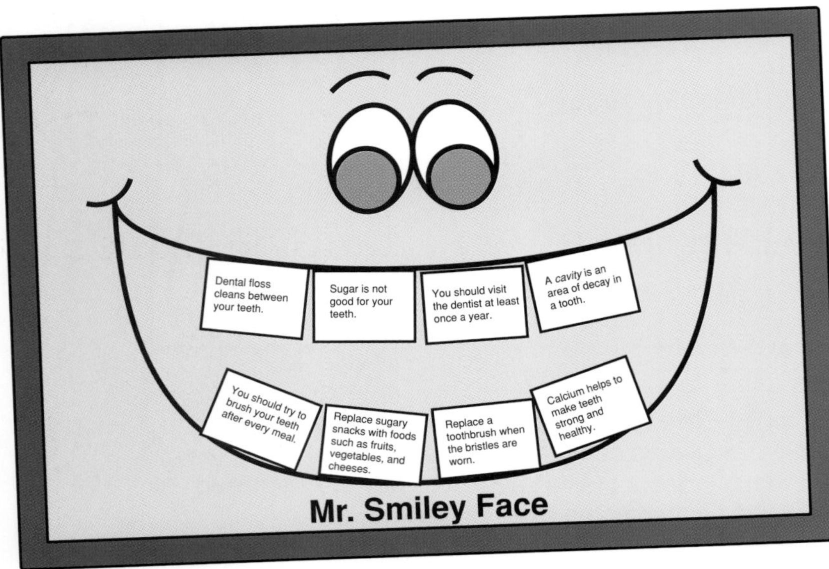

4. For further review with healthful dental-health habits, distribute a copy of page 93 to each student. As you read each statement aloud, have each student circle the "T" if the statement is true and circle the "F" if the statement is false.

5. Challenge each student to complete the Bonus Box activity.

Name ______________________________ *Recognizing healthful dental-health habits*

Tip-Top Teeth

Read each sentence.
Circle the **T** if the sentence is **true.**
Circle the **F** if the sentence is **false.**

1. Sugar is good for your teeth. **T** **F**

2. You should brush after every meal. **T** **F**

3. Dental floss cleans between your teeth and under the gum line. **T** **F**

4. You should floss your teeth once a day. **T** **F**

5. You should visit the dentist only when your teeth hurt. **T** **F**

6. Fruits, vegetables, cheeses, and nuts are good snacks for your teeth. **T** **F**

7. You should never brush your tongue. **T** **F**

8. You should use a soft toothbrush. **T** **F**

9. Milk is good for your teeth. **T** **F**

Bonus Box: On another sheet paper, work with a friend to rewrite the false sentences as true.

How To Extend The Lesson:

- Be sure that your dental-health lesson includes some of the following terrific tooth tales:
  —*The Bear's Toothache* by David McPhail (Little, Brown And Company, 1988)
  —*Arthur's Tooth* by Marc Brown (Little, Brown And Company; 1985)
  —*Dr. De Soto* by William Steig (Farrar, Straus & Giroux, Inc.; 1990)
  —*The Tooth Fairy* by Audrey Wood (Child's Play [International] Ltd., 1996)
  —*Just Going To The Dentist* by Mercer Mayer (Western Publishing Company, 1990)

- Explain to students that teeth play an important part in speech. The teeth and tongue are used together to form many sounds that make up words. For example, to make the *th* sound, the tip of the tongue is placed against the upper front teeth. A person who lacks these teeth may be unable to make the sound. After sharing this information, have students make a variety of beginning consonant sounds. Ask students to determine which letters depend on teeth to help make their sounds.

- Have students make tooth necklaces to showcase their knowledge of dental-health facts. To make a necklace, each student cuts out the teeth from page 93 that contain true statements; then she stacks the teeth cutouts together. (If desired reword the false statements so they are true, and write them on the chalkboard. Then have each student copy each statement onto a provided tooth cutout.) Hole-punch each child's cutouts; then thread a length of dental floss through the holes and tie the floss's ends together. Encourage students to wear their necklaces home and share these healthful habits with their families.

Answer Keys

Page 5

Page 21

Possible answers include:

1. have fur; are mammals; have four legs (bear picture)
2. have feathers; have beaks; have wings; are birds (eagle picture)
3. have scaly skin; are reptiles (alligator picture)
4. have six legs; are insects (grasshopper picture)

Page 29

Mammals (yes): dolphin, lion, pig, sheep, kangaroo, bat, giraffe

Not mammals (no): frog, butterfly, snake, goldfish, duck, ant

Page 77

Magnetic: iron nail, spoon (not plastic), scissors (not plastic), screw

Nonmagnetic: penny, nickel, dime, aluminum foil, crayon, key

Page 73

1. wooden pencil—floats
2. thin rubber band—floats
3. thin crayon—floats
4. paper clip—sinks
5. ruler—floats
6. chalk—sinks
7. metal scissors—sink
8. key—sinks

Page 81

Levers:

Inclined Planes:

Wheels And Axles:

Grade 1 Science Management Checklist

SKILLS	PAGES	DATE(S) USED	COMMENTS
BASIC SCIENCE SKILLS			
Living And Nonliving	3		
Adaptable Science Project	7		
PLANTS			
Parts Of A Plant	11		
Needs Of A Plant	15		
ANIMALS			
Classification	19		
Life Cycles	23		
Mammals	27		
Insects	31		
Birds	35		
WEATHER			
Seasons	39		
Clouds	43		
Temperature & Thermometers	47		
Precipitation	51		
THE EARTH			
Reducing, Reusing, & Recycling	55		
Sun And Moon	59		
Rocks And Minerals	63		
PROPERTIES OF MATTER			
States Of Matter	67		
Sink And Float	71		
Magnets	75		
SIMPLE MACHINES			
Simple Machines	79		
THE HUMAN BODY			
The Five Senses	83		
Nutrition	87		
Dental Health	91		